GILLIAN BUTLER is a Fellow of the British Psychological Society and a founder member of the Academy of Cognitive Therapy. She works both for the NHS and for Oxford Cognitive Therapy Centre. Through ten years of clinical research with the University of Oxford, she helped to develop and evaluate cognitive behavioural treatments for social phobia and for generalized anxiety disorder. She has a special clinical interest in the use of CBT during recovery from traumatic experiences in childhood and runs training workshops on a wide variety of topics relevant to practitioners of CBT, in the UK and other countries. She is particularly interested in making the products of research available to the general public and, in addition to being the author of *Overcoming Social Anxiety and Shyness*, she is co-author of *Manage Your Mind: The Mental Fitness Guide* and of *Psychology: A Very Short Introduction*.

The *Overcoming* series was initiated by PETER COOPER, Professor of Psychology at the University of Reading and Honorary NHS Consultant Clinical Psychologist. His original book on bulimia nervosa and binge-eating founded the series in 1993 and continues to help many thousands of people in the USA, the UK and Europe. The aim of the series is to help people with a wide range of common problems and disorders to take control of their own recovery programme using the latest techniques of cognitive behavioural therapy. Each book, with its specially tailored programme, is devised by a practising clinician. Many books in the *Over-coming* series are now recommended by the UK Department of Health under the Books on Prescription scheme.

Other titles in the *Overcoming* series:

3-part self-help courses

Overcoming Anxiety Self-Help Course
Overcoming Bulimia Nervosa and Binge-Eating Self-Help Course
Overcoming Low Self-Esteem Self-Help Course
Overcoming Panic and Agoraphobia Self-Help Course

Single-volume books

Overcoming Anger and Irritability
Overcoming Anorexia Nervosa
Overcoming Anxiety
Bulimia Nervosa and Binge-Eating
Overcoming Childhood Trauma
Overcoming Chronic Fatigue
Overcoming Chronic Pain
Overcoming Compulsive Gambling
Overcoming Depression
Overcoming Insomnia and Sleep Problems
Overcoming Low Self-Esteem
Overcoming Mood Swings
Overcoming Obsessive Compulsive Disorder
Overcoming Panic
Overcoming Paranoid and Suspicious Thoughts
Overcoming Problem Drinking
Overcoming Relationship Problems
Overcoming Sexual Problems
Overcoming Social Anxiety and Shyness
Overcoming Traumatic Stress
Overcoming Weight Problems
Overcoming Your Smoking Habit

OVERCOMING
SOCIAL ANXIETY
AND SHYNESS
SELF-HELP COURSE

A 3-part programme based on
Cognitive Behavioural Techniques

Part One: Understanding Social Anxiety

Gillian Butler

ROBINSON
London

Constable & Robinson Ltd
3 The Lanchesters
162 Fulham Palace Road
London W6 9ER
www.overcoming.co.uk

First published in the UK by Robinson,
an imprint of Constable & Robinson Ltd 2007

Important Note
This book is not intended as a substitute for medical advice or treatment.
Any person with a condition requiring medical attention should consult
a qualified medical practitioner or suitable therapist.

ISBN: 978-1-84529-443-4 (Pack ISBN)

ISBN: 978-1-84529-571-4 (Part One)

ISBN: 978-1-84529-572-1 (Part Two)

ISBN: 978-1-84529-573-8 (Part Three)

Printed and bound in the EU

1 3 5 7 9 10 8 6 4 2

Contents

Contents

Foreword

The *Overcoming Social Anxiety and Shyness Self-Help Course* is an adaptation of Gillian Butler's self-help book *Overcoming Social Anxiety and Shyness*. This book provided a clear account of the nature of social anxiety and its development, as well as a set of practical strategies for tackling the various components of the problem. These strategies derive from a 'cognitive-behavioural' formulation of social anxiety – that is, they are strategies designed to change the behaviour and thoughts which provoke and maintain social anxiety. The book, first published in 1999, has helped several thousand people in Britain and elsewhere with shyness and social anxiety problems and it continues to prove enormously popular. It is increasingly widely recommended by clinicians to their patients. In this new form, as a set of workbooks, it has been updated and reformatted to make it even more accessible and easy to use.

In Part One, Dr Butler provides an explanation of the nature of both social anxiety and shyness and an account of how these problems develop and affect people's lives. In Part Two, she outlines ways of reducing self-consciousness and changing unhelpful thinking and behaviour patterns. Finally, in Part Three, she offers strategies to build up self-confidence and become more assertive.

Professor Peter Cooper
University of Reading, January 2007

Note to Practitioners

This self-help course is suitable for a wide range of reading abilities and its step-by-step format makes it ideal for working through alone or with help from a friend or professional. The course is divided into three workbooks, and each contains a full supply of worksheets and charts to be filled in on the page – so there is no need for photocopying. If you do decide to photocopy this material you will need to seek the permission of the publishers to avoid a breach of copyright law.

Introduction: How to Use this Workbook

This is a self-help course for dealing with social anxiety and shyness. It has two aims:

1 To help you develop a better understanding of the problem

2 To teach you the practical skills you will need in order to change

How the course works

The *Overcoming Social Anxiety and Shyness Self-Help Course* will help you understand how social anxiety and shyness develop and what keeps them going, and then to make changes in your life so that you begin to feel more confident.

These workbooks are designed to help you work, either by yourself or with your healthcare practitioner, to overcome social anxiety and shyness. With plenty of questionnaires, charts, worksheets and practical exercises, the three parts together make up a structured course.

It is important to be realistic: doing these tasks is time-consuming and sometimes difficult; it can also be rather repetitive. The key point to remember is that the exercises and worksheets are ways of working that research has shown to be helpful for many people. You could adapt the exercises to suit yourself, or change them from time to time if that makes the tasks more interesting.

Part One explains:

- What social anxiety is

- What are its symptoms and effects

- The different kinds of social anxiety and how common it is

- What shyness is and how it links with social anxiety

- How the way you think plays a major role in social anxiety

- What causes social anxiety

- What happens when you are socially anxious – and pinpointing what needs to change.

Part Two explains:

- Some general ideas about overcoming social anxiety
- How to reduce your self-consciousness
- How to change your thinking patterns
- How to do things differently.

Part Three explains:

- How to build up confidence
- How to deal with unhelpful underlying beliefs and assumptions
- How to put what you've learnt into action and overcome any practical problems
- How to become more assertive
- How to overcome bullying in your past
- How to develop relaxation skills.

How long will the course take?

Each workbook will take at least two or three weeks to work through – but do not worry if you feel that you need to give each one extra time. Some things can be understood and changed quite quickly, but others take longer. You will know when you are ready to move on to the next workbook. Completing the entire course could take two or three months, but it could take less and it could take a lot more. This will depend on the level of your social anxiety, on how quickly you are able to work and how ready you feel to make changes in your life. Take your time, and go at the pace that suits you best. You are the best judge of what you can do at any one time. If you get stuck and need a break from the work, make sure you plan when to start again.

Getting the most from the course

Here are some tips to help you get the most from the workbooks:

- These workbooks are not precious objects to be kept on the shelf – they are practical tools. So feel free not only to write on the worksheets and charts, but also to underline and highlight things, and to write comments and questions in the margins. By the time you have finished with a workbook it should look well and truly used.

- You will also find lots of space in the main text. This is for you to write down your thoughts and ideas, and your responses to the questions.

- Keep an open mind and be willing to experiment with new ideas and skills. These workbooks will sometimes ask you to think about painful issues. However, if social anxiety is distressing you and restricting your life it really is worth making the effort to do this as it will help you to overcome it. The rewards will be substantial.

- Be prepared to invest time in doing the practical exercises – set aside 20 to 30 minutes each day if you can.

- Try to answer all the questions and do the exercises, even if you have to come back to some of them later. There may be times when you get stuck and can't think how to take things forward. If this happens don't get angry with yourself or give up. Just put the workbook aside and come back to it later when you are feeling more relaxed.

- You may find it helpful to work through the workbooks with a friend. Two heads are often better than one. And if your friend also suffers from social anxiety you may be able to encourage each other to persist, even when one of you is finding it hard.

- Use the Thoughts and Reflections section at the back of the workbook to write down anything that has been particularly helpful to you. This can be anything you read (here or elsewhere), or think, or do, or anything that someone else says to you. These pages are to help you collect together your own list of helpful ideas.

- Re-read the workbook. You may get more out of it once you've had a chance to think about some of the ideas and put them into practice for a little while.

- Each workbook builds on what has already been covered. So what you learn when working with one will help you when you come to the next. It's quite possible simply to dip into different ones as you please, but you will get most out of this series of three workbooks if you follow them through systematically, step by step.

A note of caution

These workbooks will not help everyone who has problems with social anxiety and shyness. Everyone finds it hard to turn and face a problem that troubles them and doing so can make you feel worse at first. However, a few people find that focusing on social anxiety persistently makes them feel worse instead of better. This might be because they have another problem as well. The most common problems that go with social anxiety are depression and dependence on alcohol (or non-prescribed drugs). The recognized signs of clinical depression are listed below. They include:

- Constantly feeling sad, down, depressed or empty
- General lack of interest in what's going on around you
- A big increase or decrease in your appetite and weight
- A marked change in your sleep patterns
- Noticeable speeding up or slowing down in your movements and how you go about things
- Fatigue, and feeling low in energy
- An intense sense of guilt or worthlessness
- Difficulty concentrating and making decisions
- A desire to hurt yourself or a feeling that you might be better off dead

If you have become depressed because of your social anxiety, and the depression is getting in the way of using this workbook, then it would be sensible to deal with the depression first. However, many people who feel a bit depressed from time to time find that the constructive work on solving their underlying social anxiety problem also makes them feel less unhappy.

If you have had five or more of the symptoms listed above (including low mood or loss of interest) for two weeks or more, you should seek professional help from a doctor, counsellor or psychotherapist. There is nothing shameful about seeking this sort of professional help – any more than there is anything shameful about taking your car to a garage if it is not working as it should, or going to see a lawyer if you have legal problems. It simply means taking your journey towards self-knowledge and self-acceptance with the help of a friendly guide, rather than striking out alone.

SECTION 1: What Is Social Anxiety?

This section will help you to understand:

- What social anxiety is
- Whether you suffer from social anxiety

What is social anxiety?

Social anxiety describes the fear, nervousness and apprehension most of us at times experience in our relationships with other people.

Some people who suffer from social anxiety would say they were shy, and may have been shy all their lives. But some people who are not shy also suffer from social anxiety. So shyness is not the whole story.

Social anxiety strikes people when they think that they might do something that will be humiliating or embarrassing. Social anxiety makes you think that other people are judging you, and doing so in a negative way, because of something you said or did.

Take a moment to think about a recent occasion when you worried about what other people thought of you. Describe what happened and how you felt in the space below.

_____

_____

_____

_____

_____

The fear that you will do something humiliating or embarrassing stops you from behaving naturally. It also makes you self-aware: conscious of the possibility that you might indeed do such a thing. Who would want to get into conversation if they thought that doing so would only reveal their clumsiness, or inadequacy, or tendency to blush?

Socially anxious people tend to assume that their interactions with others will be painfully revealing. You think that others will notice your weaknesses or awkwardness; that you will be dismissed, ignored, criticized or rejected for not behaving more acceptably.

The effect of social anxiety

Seeing things this way makes it hard to interact naturally with people, and difficult to talk, listen or make friends. Often it leads to isolation and loneliness. For many people one of the sadnesses of suffering from this problem is that it prevents them becoming intimate with other people, or finding a partner with whom to share their life.

How do you think social anxiety or shyness has affected your life? Write down some of your thoughts here.

Hiding your true self

Socially anxious people usually feel friendly towards others. They also have their fair share of the positive characteristics that other people appreciate. You may have a sense of humour, be energetic and generous, kind and understanding, serious, amusing, quiet or lively. What's more you naturally behave in these ways when you feel at ease.

But feeling at ease in company is so hard for socially anxious people, and makes them so anxious, that these qualities are often hidden from view. Your anxiety interferes with their expression. Also, your ability to display these qualities may have gone rusty from lack of use. Indeed, you may have altogether lost belief in your likeable qualities together with your self-confidence.

One of the rewards of learning to overcome social anxiety is that it helps you to express aspects of yourself that may have been stifled. It allows you to enjoy, rather than to fear, being yourself and rediscover exactly who you are.

List on the opposite page some of the positive qualities you have and which you can reveal when you are feeling relaxed and at ease.

My good points (strengths, qualities, talents)

_____

_____

_____

_____

_____

Warning: this is hard to do if you are feeling troubled or low. You may need to come back to this exercise several times (when you are feeling low and then when you feel more positive).

Defining the problem

Definitions are useful because they help us to focus on the features of social anxiety that make it a problem – that cause the pain and prolong the agony.

Social anxiety is normal. Everybody feels it sometimes so everyone knows to some degree what it is like. And at some stage all of us will probably feel socially anxious again.

For this reason it helps to :

- Define when social anxiety becomes a problem

- Think clearly about what it is that needs to change when it interferes with your life

Rather than attempting the impossible, and seeking a 'cure' for social anxiety, it is more useful to learn how to reduce its painful aspects and consequences, so that it no longer causes distress and interferes with your life.

Social phobia and social anxiety

Different terms are used by therapists to describe social anxiety. One term you may hear used is 'social phobia'. This term describes very similar experiences to social anxiety and shyness, although generally people who have social phobia will have more severe symptoms. The term is used by therapists to make a clinical diagnosis of problem social anxiety as opposed to normal social anxiety which, as we know, everyone experiences from time to time.

In this book we'll use the term 'social anxiety' rather than 'social phobia'. There is no hard and fast distinction between being socially anxious and having a (diagnosable) social phobia. Also social anxiety is what people with social phobia feel, so it makes sense to use the ordinary language term that refers to both conditions. And finally, the same ideas apply to understanding the problem and working out how to overcome it. This is the case whether you have mild, occasional social anxiety or a more entrenched and distressing social phobia.

Do I have social phobia or social anxiety?

Therapists have established that there are key ways of behaving or thinking that are shared by people suffering from social phobia. The questions below look at some of these key ways of behaving and thinking.

Read each question below and check the answers that apply to you. For each question there is room for you to describe your own particular experience, as social anxiety takes many different forms. Remember, answering these questions is not the same as getting a diagnosis from a therapist. But the questions may help you identify and focus on your particular problem.

Question 1

Do you fear particular social situations such as parties or situations where you have to 'perform', such as a job interview?

Place a tick in the column in the table opposite beside each situation that applies to you. If your feared situation doesn't appear in the list, write it in the space provided.

Type of social situation	Yes, definitely	Yes, mostly	Yes, sometimes	No, mostly	No, not at all
Do you fear going to parties or other social events?					
Do you fear speaking up at meetings or amongst a group of people you don't know well?					
Do you find it difficult to eat or drink in front of people you don't know well?					
Do you find it hard to start a conversation and continue it?					
Do you find it difficult to talk on the telephone?					
Do you dislike entering a room by yourself?					
Do you find it difficult to talk to an attractive person?					
Do you fear having to give a speech in public?					
Do you fear having to do things like sign your name or fill in a form while other people are watching?					
Do you have a fear of job interviews or performance reviews?					
Do you dread attracting attention?					
Other (write in)					

People who suffer from social phobia or social anxiety have a strong and persistent fear of social situations or events where they might have to 'perform' such as a job interview or speaking in public.

Such situations involve being exposed to unfamiliar people or to the possibility of being judged or observed by others.

Question 2

In these social or performance situations, do you think you will act in a way or show signs that will be humiliating or embarrassing?

Place a tick in the column below beside each way of behaving or sign that applies to you. If your symptom doesn't appear in the list, write it in the space provided.

Humiliating or embarrassing signs	Yes, definitely	Yes, mostly	Yes, sometimes	No, mostly	No, not at all
Do you fear you will become tongue-tied?					
Do you fear you will stammer or stutter?					
Do you fear you won't make any sense or will say something stupid?					
Do you fear you will blush?					
Do you fear you will sweat?					
Do you fear you will be clumsy?					
Do you fear you will talk nonsense, or say something that will make people stare at you?					
Other (write in)					

People who suffer from social anxiety or phobia fear that they will act in a way (or show anxiety symptoms) that will be humiliating or embarrassing.
It's important to note that people with social phobia may not actually do anything humiliating or embarrassing; they only have to fear that they will. Your symptoms do not even have to show. You only have to think that there is a possibility of this happening for you to feel fearful and anxious.

Question 3(a)

How frequently do you feel anxious in these social or performance situations?

Place an X on the scale below to show how frequently you feel anxious. 0 is never feeling anxious and 10 is always feeling anxious.

0	1	2	3	4	5	6	7	8	9	10
Never										Always

Question 3(b)

How anxious do you feel during these situations?

Place an X on the scale below to rate your level of anxiety. 0 is not feeling anxious at all and 10 is feeling extremely anxious.

0	1	2	3	4	5	6	7	8	9	10
Not anxious										Extremely anxious

Therapists have found that for sufferers of social anxiety or phobia being exposed to the feared situation causes a high level of anxiety almost all the time.
There is no hard and fast line between normal and clinical levels of anxiety – all degrees of social anxiety exist. But social anxiety at a normal level doesn't tend to occur frequently. The feelings come and they also go. For everyone there are likely to be some particularly bad times, for example when starting a new job and going through the ordeal of showing that you can do what is expected of you. There are also likely to be some relatively good ones, when you feel more confident and at ease.
 For people whose level of social anxiety causes them to suffer there are more bad times and fewer good ones, and the bad times are worse.

Question 4

Do you think your reaction to the social situation you fear is (tick whichever applies):

☐ **a** Unreasonable or excessive

☐ **b** A little over-the-top

☐ **c** Normal under the circumstances

People who suffer from social anxiety generally recognize that their fear is excessive and unreasonable.

One of the distressing consequences of having a social phobia is that you know that the things that make you anxious are not really dangerous, and that they may hardly bother other people at all. But knowing that you suffer 'excessively' and 'unreasonably' compared with others – that in some sense your suffering is unnecessary – only makes it worse. It can make you feel unconfident, inadequate or inferior as well as anxious.

Question 5

If a situation arises that you fear (for example, speaking in public, going to a party, having to talk to a person you don't know well) do you:

☐ **a** Do anything to avoid the situation; for example, pretend to be ill or make some other excuse to get away

☐ **b** Get through it but feel terrible – extremely anxious or distressed

☐ **c** Find as many ways you can to protect yourself or keep safe, and come away thinking you were lucky to have survived

☐ **d** Get through it and find it wasn't as bad as you imagined it would be

People who suffer from social anxiety or phobia avoid feared social or performance situations or else endure them with intense anxiety or distress.

It is only natural – it makes sense in terms of self-protection – to avoid or escape from frightening situations. The experience of fear alerts you to the possibility of danger. Staying where you are might be risky.

However, people with social anxiety are in an especially difficult position. Nobody wants to be lonely and isolated. Also, you cannot control the sources of your fear: other people and the thoughts that other people might have about you. Contact with people, when shopping, travelling or working, cannot be avoided completely, and social anxiety doesn't stop you wanting to work, make friends and feel that you belong just as much as others.

So instead of avoiding or escaping from difficult situations, you may endure them despite the distress that you feel, and focus on keeping the risks or threats as small as possible: on keeping yourself as safe as you can. The intensity of the anxiety you feel makes this strategy seem only sensible.

Both of these ways of behaving unfortunately tend to keep social anxiety going. We'll look at why this happens and how to overcome the problem later in the course.

Other features of problem social anxiety

There are some other general points that highlight the difference between normal social anxiety and **social phobia** (remember, this is the technical term for the clinical diagnosis). Tick any that you think relate to you:

- ☐ The problem must interfere with your life

- ☐ The problem must cause a significant degree of distress

- ☐ The problem must have persisted for at least six months

Whether these three points add up to social phobia is often a matter for the therapist to decide. There's no hard and fast way of deciding what degree of distress counts as significant, for example.

Two kinds of social phobia

Therapists often distinguish between two kinds of social phobia.

1 For some people the problem is relatively limited. They feel anxious in just a few situations, such as speaking in public or being with sexually attractive people. This is called **specific social phobia**.

2 For others it is more likely to affect most situations involving interaction with others. This is called **generalized social phobia**.

Shyness versus social anxiety

We could also use the term 'shyness' to describe this problem. If you are shy you will have recognized and understood many of the descriptions given above. As we shall see in Section 4, shyness is similar to social anxiety, even though it does not have the kind of technical definition that would turn it into a diagnosable condition.

More is known about social anxiety than about shyness, which psychologists have only recently started to study. However, there is much overlap between the two. The symptoms of social anxiety which are described in Section 2 are also likely to be familiar to shy people.

This does not mean that shy people should be 'diagnosed' as having a psychological disorder. Shyness as well as social anxiety comes in varying degrees, and its effects can be more or less of a problem.

The next section looks more closely at the effects of social anxiety on your day-to-day life. It will help you work out more specifically the problems you face and exactly what you want to change.

Summary

1   It is normal to feel socially anxious occasionally. Indeed, this seems to be a universal phenomenon.

2   People for whom social anxiety causes problems suppose that other people are evaluating them negatively. They also fear that they will do something in public that will be embarrassing or humiliating.

3   There are many similarities between social anxiety and shyness. This workbook will help people who suffer both a mild form of social anxiety or shyness and those who suffer more distressing and severe forms.

SECTION 2: The Symptoms and Effects of Social Anxiety

This section will help you understand:

- What are the symptoms of social anxiety

- What are the effects of social anxiety on your life

The next step in understanding social anxiety is to think in more detail about how it affects you. What are its main symptoms?

You've already done some thinking about this problem in your answers to the questions on page 6. Let's look at this more closely.

Social anxiety can affect your **thinking**, your **behaviour**, your **body** and your **emotions**. The questions below are grouped in each of those categories. It's important to remember that no two people are ever exactly the same so if you don't recognize your symptoms in the list, write them in the space provided.

It would be unusual not to have any symptoms at all in one of these four categories, although it can at first be difficult to recognize some of them in yourself. It is worth spending some time thinking through your particular experience of social anxiety, using this questionnaire as a prompt.

Signs and symptoms of social anxiety

Tick any of the questions below that apply to you. Remember, if you think of something that doesn't appear in the list write it in the space provided.

Effects on thinking

Imagine yourself in a situation that makes you socially anxious. It may be speaking up in a meeting, going to a party where you don't know anyone, or talking to someone very attractive. Do you:

☐ **a** Worry about what others think of you?

☐ **b** Find it difficult to concentrate, or remember what people say?

☐ **c** Find that you focus attention on yourself and are painfully aware of how you feel, and of what you do and say?

☐ **d**   Worry about how you are coming over?

☐ **e**   Think about what might go wrong ahead of time?

☐ **f**   Dwell on things you think you did wrong after the event?

☐ **g**   Find your mind goes blank and you're unable to think what to say?

☐ **h**   Other (write in):

_____

_____

_____

Effects on behaviour

In the same situation do you:

☐ **a**   Speak quickly or quietly, mumble and get words mixed up?

☐ **b**   Avoid catching someone's eye?

☐ **c**   Do things to make sure that you do not attract attention?

☐ **d**   Keep safe: for example, would you only talk to 'safe', non-threatening people, about 'safe' topics?

☐ **e**   Go out of your way to avoid these difficult social occasions or situations in the first place?

☐ **f**   Other (write in):

_____

_____

_____

Effects on the body

Do you:

☐ **a**   Blush?

☐ **b** Sweat?

☐ **c** Tremble or shake?

☐ **d** Feel tense; do you experience the aches and pains that go with being unable to relax?

☐ **e** Get panicky feelings: does your heart pound, do you feel dizzy, nauseous or breathless?

☐ **f** Other (write in):

_____

_____

Effects on emotions or feelings

Do you feel:

☐ **a** Nervous, anxious, fearful, apprehensive or self-conscious?

☐ **b** Frustrated and angry, with yourself and/or with others?

☐ **c** Unconfident or inferior to others?

☐ **d** Sad, or depressed, or hopeless about being able to change?

☐ **e** Envious of all those people who don't seem to have any difficulty, socially?

Everything is linked

In practice you will find that these four types of symptoms link up with each other. Thoughts, behaviours, bodily reactions and emotions (or feelings) interlink in various ways, and each of them affects all of the others.

For example, **thinking** you look foolish makes you **feel** self-conscious. So you look away, and try to fade into the background **(your behaviour)**. This makes you aware that you are trembling and your heart is thumping **(your bodily reactions)**.

Or feeling hot and panicky **(your bodily reaction)** makes it hard to **think** what to say, so you blurt out something that makes little sense **(your behaviour)**, and then **feel** embarrassed.

This interconnection between thoughts, feelings (both emotions and bodily feelings or sensations) and behaviour makes it hard to disentangle how a particular bout of anxiety first started. Section 7 (page 87) describes more about how the various aspects of social anxiety fit together.

The effects of social anxiety

Let's now look at what it's like to have social anxiety and its wide-ranging effects.

Avoidance

One common way in which people cope with social anxiety is to avoid the feared situation. We simply don't do something because to do it would make us anxious. Therapists call this behaviour **avoidance** and it can have powerful effects on your life.

Avoidance can take very obvious forms. For example some socially anxious people avoid going out with friends, to meetings or to grander social occasions such as weddings. These people know that in doing this they are leading a more restricted social life than they would like, but feel unable to face the strain of the event.

Other socially anxious people continue to go to events that they fear. On the surface it seems that their lives are not restricted and that avoidance is not a problem for them. However, there are many subtle ways in which you can avoid difficult aspects of situations. Tick any of the questions below that apply to you.

Do you:

☐ **a** Wait for someone else to arrive before entering a room full of people?

☐ **b** Hand things round at a party, so as to avoid getting into conversation?

☐ **c** Avoid getting into conversation?

☐ **d** Put things off, such as meeting the neighbours or shopping at crowded times?

☐ **e** Turn away when you see someone coming who makes you feel anxious?

☐ **f** Avoid talking about anything personal with colleagues or people you don't know well?

☐ **g** Avoid using your hands when others might be watching?

☐ **h** Not eat in public places?

Can you think of any other ways in which you avoid a feared situation? Write them down here.

_____

_____

_____

It's worth remembering...

If you avoid something, you cannot learn that it is harmless.

If you're always handing things round at a party, how can you get used to talking to new people? Or if you never talk about personal things, how can people get to know you well?

It is important not to overlook subtle kinds of avoidance as, like avoidance of more obvious kinds, they play an important part in keeping the problem going. Later in the course (page 97) we'll look at strategies for dealing with avoidance.

Safety behaviours

Other people are the problem for people who are socially anxious. One of the difficulties about other people is that you can never predict what they will do next. At any moment they may, unwittingly perhaps, 'land you in it': that is, they may do precisely the thing that you find hardest to deal with.

For example, they might:

- Put you on the spot by asking you a direct question

- Introduce you to the person who makes you feel most anxious (someone in authority or the most attractive person in the room)

- Ask for your opinion

- Or they might just walk away from you to talk to someone else.

So when you are with other people you can feel constantly at risk – and it is not at all clear what you could avoid to make yourself feel better. When this happens your mind naturally focuses on how to keep safe.

Socially anxious people develop a wide range of 'safety behaviours', or things that they do in order to reduce the sense of being at risk. Many safety behaviours involve trying not to attract unwanted attention.

Read the questions below and tick any in the list below that apply to you.

Do you:

☐ **a** Look at the floor so that no one can catch your eye?

☐ **b** If you're a woman, wear heavy make-up to hide your blushes?

☐ **c** Wear light clothing in case you feel hot and sweaty?

☐ **d** Leave the room immediately a meeting is over so that you do not have to get involved in 'small talk'?

☐ **e** Rehearse what you are about to say, mentally checking you have got the words right?

☐ **f** (i) Speak slowly, or quietly? or
(ii) Talk fast, not stopping to draw breath?

☐ **g** (i) Hide your hands or face? or (ii) Put your hand to your mouth?

☐ **h** Hold things tight, or lock your knees together to control shaking?

☐ **i** (i) Let your hair fall in front of your face? or (ii) Wear clothes that hide parts of your body?

☐ **j** (i) Try to amuse people and tell jokes? or
(ii) Never risk a joke?

☐ **k** (i) Not talk about yourself or your feelings? or (ii) Never express opinions?

☐ **l** Say nothing that might be challenging or controversial, you always agree with everyone?

☐ **m** (i) Wear smart clothes that give you a protective 'armour' or 'veneer'? or
(ii) Wear unnoticeable clothes (so as not to stand out)?

☐ **n** Stick with a 'safe' person or in a 'safe' place; you never take any chances?

☐ **o** Keep an eye on the escape route; you never get fully involved?

Can you think of any other ways in which you try to keep yourself safe?

_____

_____

_____

As you worked through these questions you may have noticed that some of them appear to be opposites. For example, either keeping quiet or trying to keep the conversation going.

This is because different people want to do different things in order to feel safe. It may feel safer to say little, and to make sure that what you do say makes sense. That way you feel as if you can reduce the risk of making a fool of yourself.

Or you may feel safer if you take responsibility for keeping a conversation going. When a silence feels like eternity it can feel safer to keep on chattering even if you might not be making a lot of sense.

Like avoidance, safety behaviours can keep social anxiety going. We'll look at strategies to deal with this in Part Two, Section 4.

Dwelling on the problem

Social anxiety can come upon you, and feel overwhelming when it does, at the drop of a hat. This may partly happen because other people are unpredictable. It may also happen because the fear of being anxious is constantly on your mind. Therapists call this **anticipatory anxiety**.

Thinking about future encounters can bring to your mind a host of thoughts about how things might go wrong. This can often be in rather vague and threatening ways:

- 'What if I can't think of anything to say?'

- 'What if everyone else knows people but I don't?'

- 'What if I'm expected to speak up?'

- 'What if my voice starts to tremble?'

You might like to write in your own 'what if' thoughts here about a situation you fear:

_____

_____

Apprehension and worry make it hard to look forward to events that others enjoy or find relaxing, such as the drink after the football game, the lunch break at work, going to a party or visiting a friend.

Worrying after the event

Even when the event is over your mind can be prey to further anxiety. Many people constantly turn over thoughts, images and memories of what happened. It's as if you need to do a post mortem like airport authorities do after a 'near miss' on the runway.

Socially anxious people tend to dwell on their interactions with others as if they were narrowly averted catastrophes. You may focus on something that you think you did 'wrong', or that did not feel quite right, or that embarrassed you.

You may also make assumptions about other people's reactions, including their private and unexpressed opinions. These assumptions tend to place you in a negative light, so the post mortem after even a brief, uneventful interaction can bring on a bout of self-criticism: 'I'm hopeless – useless – too anxious to pay attention or think straight – stupid – different from everyone else – inept.' Socially anxious people can be extremely hard on themselves.

In the space below write about a recent event that you felt upset about. Describe what you thought about this afterwards. How did it make you feel about yourself? What do you think the other people present thought of you? What do you remember doing? We'll be challenging some of your ideas about yourself and others later in the course.

The problem with the post mortem

We all sometimes do something that embarrasses or humiliates us. We all have memories of a few things that make us cringe, blush, curl up or want to hide when we think of them. Remembering these things can bring back all the dreadful feelings with which you were engulfed at the time – even if it happens at four o'clock in the morning and no one can see your blushes.

There is nothing 'abnormal' about the post mortem itself. It probably reflects the way we handle other intense or distressing experiences. We usually go over such things in our minds many times before we can absorb them, adjust accordingly and move on, leaving the distress behind.

The post mortem is a reflection of the suffering we experience with social phobias. But, as we shall see below, it keeps the suffering going rather than resolving it.

The post mortems conducted by people who suffer from social anxiety are largely based on what they think happened, and not on what actually happened; on what they think other people thought of them rather than on what they actually thought. They are unnecessary because they are based on guesswork, not fact.

Take a look again at how you described a recent distressing event above. How much of what you wrote is based on guesswork and how much on provable facts? Write down your thoughts here.

_____

_____

_____

You will learn more about how to distinguish facts and opinions in Part Two, Section 2.

Self-esteem, self-confidence and feelings of inferiority

Social anxiety makes you feel different from other people in a negative way – less good than them, or odd. This is in turn means it comes to affect your self-esteem (sense of self-worth) as well as your self-confidence (belief in your ability to do things).

You come to expect that people will ignore or reject you. You tend to interpret the things that they do, like the way they look at you or speak to you, as signs that they think badly of you. You feel at risk of being on the receiving end of their criticism or negative evaluation. You feel you will be found wanting in some way – as if your weaknesses or inadequacies were about to be revealed.

Write down here your thoughts about how you think social anxiety may have affected your self-esteem.

_____

_____

_____

You may live with a constant undercurrent of fear, and with the sense that you are lurching from one lucky escape to the next. Many socially anxious people think that others would reject them outright if they only knew what they were really like. You may go to great lengths to hide your 'real self', even though there is nothing wrong with you other than feeling anxious. Of course, this makes it hard to express an opinion or to say how you feel about something.

Write down here some ways in which you think you hide your real self:

_____

_____

_____

_____

_____

Socially anxious people may also suppose that other people are never socially anxious. They think that they have fewer, or less socially revealing, weaknesses and inadequacies; or that they are able to go through life without feeling nervous about how others think of them. In fact everyone feels nervous in social situations sometimes, so you really aren't alone. And at the other extreme it can cause just as many problems to be insensitive to others as it does to be too sensitive to them.

Demoralization and depression; frustration and resentment

It feels frustrating to stifle parts of your personality, so not surprisingly, persistent social anxiety gets you down. It can make you feel demoralized or depressed as well as anxious or angry. You may feel resentful that others seem to find easy so many things that for you are very difficult. Anxiety is by no means the only emotion associated with social anxiety.

Write down here how your social anxiety makes you feel:

_____

_____

_____

_____

Effects on performance

The difficulty about high levels of anxiety – whatever causes them – is that they inter-fere with activities and with the ability to put plans into action. They make it harder for you to perform to the best of your ability, and prevent you achieving the things that you want to achieve.

A certain amount of anxiety is helpful if you have to go for an interview, or sit an examination: it can energize and motivate you, and help to focus your mind. But more than that becomes preoccupying and makes it hard to behave as you otherwise would, or hard to do your best.

So in the short term social anxiety stops people doing what they want to do, and might otherwise be capable of doing. In the long term this can have a wide range of different effects, on careers, personal relationships, friendships, work and leisure activities.

Describe here some of the effects you think social anxiety has had on your life, both in the short term and in the long term.

Effects on my career:

_____

_____

_____

_____

_____

Effects on my personal relationships:

_____

_____

_____

_____

_____

Effects on my friendships:

_____

_____

_____

_____

Effects on my leisure activities:

_____

_____

_____

_____

Other effects:

_____

_____

_____

_____

_____

It may have been distressing to think in such detail about the effect of social anxiety on your life. But it is only by identifying the particular symptoms and problems you face that you can start to work out exactly what needs to change.

This self-help course will help you change the effect of social anxiety on your life. By working through the exercises in Parts One, Two and Three you will begin to turn things around and start to live the life you want to live.

Summary

1 There are four different kinds of symptoms of social anxiety: these affect thinking, behaviour, the body, and emotions or feelings.

2 Socially anxious people avoid difficult situations, try to keep themselves safe, worry about what might happen before the event and about what did happen afterwards.

3 They may feel angry, depressed or inferior as well as anxious.

4 Social anxiety can interfere with all aspects of life: professional as well as personal.

SECTION 3: The Different Kinds of Social Anxiety and How Common It Is

This section will help you understand:

- The different kinds of social anxiety
- Common misunderstandings about social anxiety
- How many people suffer from social anxiety
- Differences in social anxiety from culture to culture.

Social anxiety may be limited to one main aspect of your life, such as eating or speaking in public. Or it may be more widespread, and have more general effects.

Work-based social anxiety

Some people cope reasonably well at work until they are offered the kind of promotion that would make them more 'visible', or require them to manage others. You might even be unable to accept the promotion because:

- It would involve attending meetings at which you would have to account for your department's activities or make presentations
- You would have to attend a training course
- You would have to organize, oversee and take responsibility for the work of others.

You may refuse promotion and remain in jobs that are well below your capabilities, so that you fail to realize much of your potential.

Or you might be able to operate well at work, even in high-profile professional jobs or in ones that are socially demanding like being a salesperson or working in public relations. You may have few difficulties as long as you are 'protected' by the conventions that surround you in the workplace. You feel fine in the lab, computer room or operating theatre.

But you may still feel at a loss in unstructured social gatherings or when your role is not clearly defined, and find it difficult to make friends – and particularly difficult to make 'small talk'. Despite considerable success at work, you may still feel lonely and isolated, and your social anxiety means that sometimes you miss out on opportunities for forming close and intimate relationships as well.

How does social anxiety affect you at work? Write down your thoughts here.

_____

_____

_____

_____

_____

Dating anxiety

Many people suffer severely from what has been called 'dating anxiety'. A degree of anxiety is very common and entirely normal in these situations; we are all anxious to impress someone we like on a first date.

However, people who suffer with this particular form of social anxiety go through extreme difficulties when they are with someone they find attractive. They become unable to put themselves across, for example, or are unable to do those things that would help them to get to know the person they feel strongly about. They can be terrified of showing they care.

If this kind of anxiety is a problem for you, write down your thoughts here.

_____

_____

_____

_____

Making new friends or moving on

Other people may have one or two good friends, and feel comfortable most of the time within the circle of those that they know well: when with their partners, or surrounded by their families. For them social anxiety interferes with meeting new people, moving to new places, or seeking out new ways of fulfilling themselves, and their lives can become painfully limited and restricted.

If this kind of anxiety is a problem for you, write down your thoughts here.

_____

_____

_____

_____

As we can see social anxiety has many faces. The strategies in this book will help you overcome all the different forms this problem can take.

Some common misunderstandings about social anxiety

There are two other kinds of anxiety that are different from social anxiety, even though they look similar at first sight: performance anxiety and stage fright.

Performance anxiety

Someone who is affected by this kind of anxiety generally wants to be able to produce their best performance – or at least a good one – when it really matters. They want to come up to the mark in their own estimation. Other people's evaluation of the performance may therefore be less important to people with performance anxiety than their own evaluation of it. They may be absolutely certain of their technique, and of their ability to produce a performance of the standard they wish. However, they are fearful that the pressures of the actual performance will interfere with this ability. This makes this kind of anxiety different from social anxiety.

Stage fright

Stage fright is probably a version of performance anxiety, and this sudden burst of fear can be totally paralysing when it occurs. But it is specific to people who give public performances, and may occur in those who are otherwise socially confident and only have this problem when they have to perform.

People who appear never to feel shy or self-conscious

Many of us believe that people who are able to give public performances, and actors in particular, are not socially anxious. We assume that they would never be able to forget themselves sufficiently to get up in front of other people, and put themselves on display, if doing so caused terrible thoughts about what other people thought of them, and aroused all the signs and symptoms of anxiety that can be so distressing.

But this seems to be wrong. Many actors, and others who provide different kinds of performances in public, may still be shy or anxious in other social situations, but able to hide their anxiety, or shyness, while 'in role'. They may also intentionally adopt a role, rather as others use safety behaviours, to help them out of a potential social difficulty.

How common is social phobia and social anxiety?

It is difficult to accurately estimate how widespread problems such as social phobia are. As we've already seen, therapists often have to make fine clinical judgments about who suffers from it to the point where it interferes with their life and who doesn't.

The studies that are now available suggest that between 3 and 13 per cent of the population will suffer from severe social anxiety at some point in their lives. That is, they suffer from a form of social anxiety that would qualify for them to be diagnosed with social phobia. The reason there is such a wide range in the estimate of sufferers is because the studies use slightly different methods and have been done at different times in different places.

Differences between men and women

In most countries the problem appears to affect men and women equally often. However, the form that it takes may differ between the sexes, partly depending on cultural factors.

For example, it used to be (and possibly still is) much harder for men than for women to seek help for psychological difficulties. It is also generally easier for men than for women to use alcohol to boost their social courage. Many specialists in treatment of alcohol-related problems have observed that social anxiety appears to contribute to the development of these problems. People report drinking, or using other substances, to reduce the anxiety they experience socially, and when problems with addiction resolve, the social anxiety may remain, or re-emerge.

Do you use alcohol or other substances to mask social anxiety? Describe how you use it here.

_____

_____

_____

_____

_____

_____

You'll find more information about the use of alcohol and social anxiety in Part Two, page 9.

There are probably many ways of masking a problem of social anxiety, and of course the anxiety itself makes people reluctant to talk about the problem. Our present estimates of how common social anxiety is may be too low.

Shyness and social anxiety

It is interesting that 40 per cent of the adult population of America describe themselves as 'shy', even though we are not quite sure what they might mean by this. They could be referring to:

- Normal levels of social anxiety, for example feeling anxious at a job interview or on a first date

- Feeling sensitive in the presence of others

- Their memory of the normal stage of shyness through which most children pass and to its occasional shadow in adult life

- Something else such as feeling generally unconfident.

But we do know that shyness is more common than social anxiety, and the nature and effects of shyness are described in more detail in Section 4.

Differences between cultures

Social anxiety is found all over the world. Its nature varies a bit with local customs, but people everywhere can worry about the possibility of doing something that might be embarrassing or humiliating for them. Exactly what that will be depends on where they are, who they are with and the conventions that have grown up in that place at that time.

For example, what might be thought of as hot-headed displays of emotion are common in Mediterranean countries. However, they are relatively rare in Nordic countries, where they might be misunderstood or attract unwanted attention.

Ways of behaving that would provoke feelings of shame in Japan might go unnoticed in America, and vice versa. For example, making too much eye contact too soon can be embarrassing in Japan, whereas for an American person not looking directly at the person to whom you are talking, especially if you have just met them, or if they are in some way important to you, might suggest that you have something to hide.

The point is that there is no single set of social conventions but many different 'socially acceptable' ways of behaving, depending on where you are. Even in the same place, these will differ depending on whether you are 18 or 80. This self-help course will help you to learn ways to feel more relaxed and confident whatever the social conventions you find yourself operating within.

Summary

1   The exact form that social anxiety takes varies from person to person, from place to place and from time to time.

2   There is no need to know exactly what causes social anxiety in order to be able to change.

SECTION 4: About Shyness

This section will help you understand:

- The similarities and the differences between shyness and social anxiety
- The symptoms of shyness
- The effects of shyness
- The advantages of shyness
- The connection between shyness and not wanting to be rude
- How shyness varies from culture to culture.

Describing shyness and its effects is different from describing social anxiety. There is no such thing as a diagnosis of shyness. This means that there is no agreed list of common features of shyness as there is in social anxiety or phobia (see page 4 for a reminder of the key features of social anxiety).

Nevertheless, in some ways shyness may be easier to understand than social anxiety or social phobia because it is so common, especially in adolescence and early adulthood. Most people have been through stages of shyness, often of an extremely painful nature. They know, or can easily remember, the fear and nervousness with which they approached all sorts of social situations when feeling shy.

Shyness has recently been studied in more detail, mostly in America, and the findings from these studies provide much useful information about the nature of shyness and its effects. Here are some of the key findings.

Facts and figures about shyness

Research teams have found that:

- Only about 5 per cent of adults believe they have never been shy at all.
- About 80 per cent of people say that they experienced periods of pronounced shyness during childhood and adolescence.
- About half the people who were shy when they were young grow out of the problem to a large degree, though a sizeable proportion of them remain shy in some situations.

- About 40 per cent of adults in America still describe themselves as shy, and in California there is some recent evidence that this number is slowly increasing.

Shyness, it appears, is not dying away. On the contrary, it is posing more people problems than it used to.

Why are more people suffering from shyness?

The reasons for this increase in the number of people for whom shyness is a problem are not properly understood yet. One possibility, of course, is that such things are gradually becoming easier to talk about, so more people admit that it is a problem for them. However, some researchers have suggested there are certain factors in modern life that could also play a role.

Technological changes

It has been suggested that people get less practice nowadays at certain kinds of social interactions than they used to. Many activities that once depended on direct communication with someone else, such as withdrawing money from a bank, filling the car up with petrol or making a complicated telephone call, can now be carried out successfully without interacting directly with anyone else.

Today, buying groceries usually involves checking a mental (or real) list while filling up a trolley. In the past we had to ask the shop assistant to find the things on the list for us. This created an opportunity to carry on a conversation, and develop a relationship, with the person supplying the goods you needed.

At work, many people spend much of their day, whether they are carrying out complex business transactions or routine, repetitive tasks, face to face with a computer screen rather than another person. Business and social interactions, including making contact with people who have similar interests, or even just chatting, can be conducted over the Internet using a keyboard, screen and mouse.

A different kind of communication

This kind of communication doesn't help people to overcome their initial shyness and to develop their confidence when meeting people face to face. Such interactions also obey completely different sets of conventions about how to communicate, and require specific skills and knowledge of new 'languages'.

Although these new methods of communication are in some ways extremely successful (fascinating and seductive too), there are many things that they do not demand.

- You don't have to be polite or friendly, or sensitive to how someone else is feeling and how their feelings change.

- You don't have to be aware of what might lie behind the communications you receive, or of what it means to others to be in contact with you.

- The person you are communicating with doesn't have to be able to laugh with you, or look at you.

- You don't have to spell things out. Texting, for example reduces communication to its bare essentials.

For someone who feels shy or wary about doing these things, or who fears that they might be being evaluated or judged or criticized when they do, this may be a relief. It is unlikely that using a computer would make someone self-conscious – that is, unless they were being watched as they used it.

But instead of easing communication between people, these forms of communication tend to leave users isolated, in social terms, from each other – able to have 'virtual' rather than real conversations.

The communication may well succeed in its own way, and is often interesting and enjoyable. But it leaves people short of practice when it comes to picking up the subtle cues with which face-to-face interactions with people are filled, and from which social confidence grows.

The bottom line

The contribution of technology to changing patterns of shyness may be exaggerated, and other factors may also be at work. However, the important point to remember is that shyness is the norm rather than the exception in early life, and that somewhere in the process of growing up, it normally lessens. It affects nearly everyone to some degree in early childhood, but continues to affect less than half the adult (American) population.

It is clear that there are some things that can hasten this change to gaining greater social confidence, and others – like relying on the Internet, email and text messaging – that might delay it. Learning more about what shyness is, and about its effects, is likely to be helpful.

How do you prefer to communicate?

It may be useful to monitor your own level of electronic communication by answering the questions below. Place a tick beside the answer that best applies to you.

1 If you need to contact a friend about meeting up do you prefer to:

- **a** Pick up the phone and call them
- **b** Send them an email or a text message
- **c** It depends on the friend

2 A colleague tells you she has a problem with some work you've sent her. Do you:

- **a** Arrange a meeting with your colleague to sort it out face to face
- **b** Ring her up – you find it easier to do that sort of thing over the phone
- **c** Send them a long and detailed email explaining yourself and what you see as the solution to the problem

3 A neighbour repeatedly plays loud music late at night. Do you:

- **a** Knock on their door the next morning and politely ask if they could keep the music down after 11pm
- **b** Thump the ceiling, floor or wall to let them know you're being disturbed
- **c** Leave them a note or send them a text message

4 Your preferred method of finding new relationships is:

- **a** To join clubs or take part in activities you enjoy and get to know people there
- **b** Hope that a friend might introduce you to someone new
- **c** To join an internet dating site

If you answered mainly b's and c's you might want to consider taking more opportunities to interact with people face to face to help build your social skills. We'll help show you how to do this in Part Two, Section 3 and Part Three, Section 1.

Is shyness a form of social anxiety, or is it something different?

A simple answer to this question is that there appear to be both similarities and differences between shyness and social anxiety. However, the two types of social difficulty have not been studied equally long, and some of the finer points have yet to be determined. So this is a question that you may have to answer for yourself by reading through this chapter and the previous one and thinking about the precise form that your problem takes.

Shyness has been said to run the whole gamut from mild social awkwardness to extreme forms of withdrawal and inhibition that are like social phobia. However, one of the main differences between people who are shy and people who are socially anxious appears to be that, at least for a proportion of people, shyness can be a passing phenomenon.

Shyness can last for a few months or years in childhood or it can re-emerge during adolescence. It is also possible that it continues in an intermittent way, so that, for example, it disappears once the 'warm-up' phase in a relationship or interaction is over. Many people who are shy to start with experience little or no social anxiety once they have overcome their initial nervousness.

Symptoms of shyness

Shyness appears always to involve a sense of shrinking back from social encounters, and of retreating into yourself. Perhaps for this reason the main symptoms of shyness are closely similar to those of social anxiety described on page 6. They include:

- Physical discomfort, such as muscle tension, sweating or trembling

- Psychological discomfort, such as feeling anxious or nervous

- Inhibition, that is being unable to express yourself freely

- Excessive self-focus, and being preoccupied with thoughts, feelings and physical reactions.

These symptoms may translate into a powerful sense of doing things wrong. It is as if everyone else knew what was required of you and knew how to decode the signals correctly. It can leave people feeling exposed, dreading the next moment, full of nervous tension, unable to forget the thumping heartbeat and the hot, red face.

The key beliefs of shy people reflect this sense of vulnerability. They tend to feel – or believe they are judged by others to be – inadequate, unlovable or unattractive.

The way in which other people react to your shyness can make a difference to the symptoms too. The more it appears to bother them, the longer your shyness may last and the worse it may feel.

Common situations when shyness is a problem

Shyness is most likely to be a problem in three types of situation:

1 When meeting someone new.

2 When interacting with people in a position of authority.

3 In one-to-one situations, especially when these involve talking to a sexually attractive person.

Shy people usually find their symptoms more intense at the following times:

- As the intimacy of a relationship increases

- When they find that they are expected to initiate activities for a group of people

- When they wish to assert themselves. This is particularly likely to be difficult if they are feeling angry or irritated, as shy people generally prefer to avoid having open disagreements. They may also be uncertain of their ability to control their feelings (positive or negative) once they start to allow them full expression.

Do you find it difficult to assert yourself? Describe a recent experience from your work or social life and what happened. How did you behave?

_____

_____

_____

_____

_____

Part Three, Section 4 will teach you techniques to help you become more assertive in these situations.

Different kinds of shyness

There are some grounds for making a distinction between two slightly different kinds of shyness.

A child's wariness

The first of these types of shyness is the sense of wariness that children start to show with strangers at a very young age. It makes good sense, in evolutionary terms, to be wary of strangers. It may help children remain cautious and safe from potential harm. This could be one reason why the childhood form of shyness is so common and so universal. It occurs in all cultures, and there seems to be no way of preventing it happening, or indeed any need to prevent it happening.

Most children outgrow this kind of shyness, at least to a large extent. It is possible that people who do not have sufficient opportunity during childhood to find out how to interact with strangers, and to learn how to work out whether they are 'safe' or 'dangerous', take longer to do this than others. Obviously there are family resemblances at work here too. In Section 6 we look in more detail at the many factors that contribute to causing social anxiety and shyness.

Being inhibited and fearing being judged

The second form of shyness is more closely related to social anxiety. Its main features are inhibition (being unable to express yourself freely) and concern about being evaluated or judged by other people.

This form is rooted in being sensitive to what you think other people thing of you. It is possible that it develops later and is more likely to occur in those people for whom the 'wariness' form of shyness is slow to fade.

However, we do not as yet know whether most shy people suffer from both kinds of shyness. Nor do we know enough about the normal course of these forms of shyness, especially in people who go on to suffer from social anxiety or social phobia. So it's unclear whether this distinction of the two forms of shyness is useful in practical terms. We'll need more research to know if it can help us to overcome forms of shyness that continue to pose problems later in life.

Shyness and introversion

As we've seen, wariness and inhibition are the key features of shyness. This should not be confused with the tendency of some people to prefer to spend time by themselves. This is called **introversion** and it's helpful to understand a little more about it.

Introverts and extroverts

People who in general prefer solitary to social activities are called **introverts**. People who tend to prefer spending time with other people are called **extroverts**. Introverts do not seek out the excitement of social interactions so often as extroverted people do. Instead they find satisfaction in activities in which they can absorb themselves regardless of whether they have someone to interact with at the time.

Of course, everyone sometimes likes to spend time alone and sometimes likes to be with people. But researchers have found that people generally tend more towards introversion or extroversion.

The difference between social anxiety and introversion

Introverts differ from people who are socially anxious. For introverts social life is not something that makes them fearful and nervous so much as something that plays a different part in their lives. Introverts can form close friendships and make intimate relationships without particular difficulty when they are interested in doing so. They seek out solitude and opportunities for independent activity not because they are lonely or isolated but because that is their style.

So shy people, and socially anxious ones too, may be either introverted or extroverted. Their natural style may be more or less sociable, and the form that their anxiety problem takes may be somewhat different depending on what they would really prefer their social life to be like.

For a shy extrovert it may be relatively easy to become involved in sociable activities that are well structured such as team sports or committee meetings. When activities are structured they know what is expected of them and are less fearful of doing something 'wrong'. It may be more difficult for them to become involved in more intimate or less structured situations.

A shy person who is introverted may suffer less than a shy extrovert, as many of the activities that they enjoy and find satisfying can be carried out alone.

The effects of shyness

The studies on shyness available so far show that its main effects are similar to the main effects of social anxiety. Read the statements below and place a tick beside any of them you feel apply to you.

The main effects of shyness

☐ Self-consciousness and self-awareness

☐ Thoughts about being evaluated negatively, and of being judged or criticized

☐ Beliefs about being inadequate, unlovable or unattractive*

☐ Avoidance and withdrawal; a sense of inward shrinking; not getting involved

☐ Finding it hard to take the initiative or to be assertive

☐ Feeling anxious, apprehensive, frustrated or unhappy when in the company of others

☐ Physical symptoms such as blushing and other signs of nervousness

*NB: Shy people are **not** less attractive, less intelligent or less competent than other people, but they may think that they are.

Indirect effects of shyness

Shyness can also have some indirect effects.

Clumsiness

When feeling shy, people can become so self-conscious and preoccupied with themselves and their feelings that they are no longer able to pay proper attention to their surroundings or to what they are doing. That is when they do something clumsy like knocking over a drink, or stumbling over a step, or bumping into a chair or table.

Shy people are normally no more clumsy than anyone else. But they become so at the worst possible times for them, when they least want to draw attention to themselves and would far prefer to appear less awkward than they feel.

Is clumsiness a problem for you? Write down a recent experience and how it made you feel.

_____

_____

_____

_____

_____

Self-esteem

It is interesting that shy children suffer fewer disadvantages from their shyness than you might expect. Their self-esteem remains unaffected at first, and so does their ability to form friendships. However, when shyness continues then the problem appears to interfere more with people's lives.

Let's look at daily activities as an example of this. Think about your current job, or if you don't work now, think about how you spend your time. Place a tick against any of the statements below that are true for you now.

☐ **1** Overall I don't really enjoy what I do

☐ **2** In general I don't think what I do allows me to take full advantage of my real potential

☐ **3** I know I could be earning more money or being more actively involved in things, but I just haven't had the breaks or the opportunities

☐ **4** I think I'm worth more than people give me credit for

Studies have shown that all of these statements tend to be true for people who remain shy into adulthood. As a consequence perhaps, many of them do suffer later on from lowered self-esteem. A few people also suffer from another secondary effect of long-lasting shyness that may be rather surprising.

Shyness and health

Studies have shown that shy adults tend to have more problems with their physical health than might otherwise be expected.

It has been suggested that this is because their shyness makes it hard for them to confide in others and to talk about their personal problems, or things that many people are sensitive or easily embarrassed about. Therefore they may delay seeking treatment when they need it, and receive less professional advice than they need. They may also receive less support from the people around them when something stressful or distressing happens to them.

Psychological research tells us that two things in particular help people to overcome all sorts of problems:

- Having a good support network

- Being able to express your feelings, whether face to face with someone else or in some other way such as by writing or through music, poetry or physical activity.

Self-expression helps people recover more quickly than keeping things to yourself. People who are able to do this suffer less from the fatigue that usually goes with persistent stress or distress, and apparently also become less vulnerable to minor illnesses.

How do you cope?

How much do you express your problems and difficulties? Make a list here of the ways that you express yourself when upset or troubled. Are there people you could talk to about your problems or difficulties. If so, list them here.

_____

_____

_____

_____

_____

_____

_____

_____

_____

_____

_____

Shame and blame

Many shy people feel ashamed of themselves for being shy – as if it were their fault, and they were to blame for not having overcome the problem. This is despite the fact that in most cases shy people continue to do things that they find difficult. Many shy people even wage a determined campaign against their shyness.

Just like people who are socially anxious, shy people tend to ignore or discount their successes. They tend to think of times when things went well for them socially as 'lucky escapes'. They remember, and tend to dwell on, any information that fits with their sense of being awkward or inadequate.

Shy people are likely to interpret ambiguous remarks made to them or about them, such as 'You seem to be rather quiet', as if they were criticisms. They also remember such remarks better than people who are not shy. They go through life expecting other people to be critical of them, and if they are asked to describe themselves they come up with more negative and fewer positive judgments than other people would.

Take the time now to list some compliments you've received in the past or successes that you've had in any area of your life. No matter how small or unimportant they seem to you, write them down and keep adding to the list as other things occur to you. Whether it was a compliment on a cake you baked, or positive feedback at work, or something good that happened when you were at school, write it down. Make a point of doing this from now on.

Advantages of shyness

Given the wide-ranging effects of shyness it may seem surprising that it also has some substantial advantages.

A mystery to be solved

Shyness is an attractive quality to many people. It can be difficult to get to know someone who is shy. But the difficulty, far from putting people off, can make people interested to know more, as if there were a mystery to be solved. The process of getting to know a shy person holds unexpected rewards.

The feel-good factor

A shy person can gradually warm to the attention they are given, and open up as they begin to feel more confident. When this happens the other person giving the attention can feel that they have won a valued confidence. It can also make that person feel good about themselves for being sensitive and attentive.

Admirable qualities

Shyness is closely related to that much-admired characteristic of the British: reserve. Shyness can also go with a gentle modesty that is the opposite of some less admired characteristics such as arrogance, loudness, being self-opinionated, pushy or conceited.

Do you think shyness can be attractive? Write down your thoughts here.

_____

_____

_____

_____

_____

_____

_____

So is there anything wrong with shyness?

Many people believe that there is nothing actually wrong with shyness. In fact some people quite consciously take advantage of the fact that it can be a very attractive quality. They may use their shyness (real or 'enhanced', perhaps) to make people curious about them.

Shyness can be an invitation, used to draw people in: a clue that there are hidden qualities to be discovered, or a mystery to be unravelled. People take advantage of their shyness in various ways. In fact they can even be accused, if they flutter their eyelashes too much, of being manipulative when they do so. In this case often the intention is not to produce a desired reaction in someone else. It's more to give themselves a helping hand in picking up the social cues or clues in a new or unfamiliar situation.

Do you ever 'exaggerate' your shyness to help you out in a social situation? Describe some of the things you do here. How do they help you?

_____

_____

_____

_____

_____

Being shy, and holding back until you feel confident enough to join in, is safer than being bold or uninhibited. This is especially the case if you fear doing the wrong thing socially and need time to get your social bearings. For example, by holding back a little you can find out who is who and how you should react to them. You can avoid making the mistake of sitting in someone else's place, or finishing up the last of the strawberries.

Can you have too little shyness?

It is also possible that having too little shyness in your make-up might be just as bad as having too much. A certain amount of shyness may apply the brakes on putting yourself forward. This may be particularly important in situations in which one person finds another attractive, and wants to make this clear. In this case a little reserve may be needed in order to check whether the other person welcomes this attention and whether the time or place is appropriate.

The ability to turn a social contact into a 'real', emotional connection, and, for example, to make people laugh or to tell jokes, is almost universally valued socially. But it is still important to be able to judge what is appropriate when. People who do not suffer from shyness at all may not pay attention to such considerations. They may say or do some 'outrageous' things which can be so embarrassing to people who are shy that they can hardly bear to be near them – or even to watch them on the television.

Do you know people who embarrass you by their 'over-the-top' behaviour? Describe how they behave and why it bothers you.

_____

_____

_____

_____

A question of balance

A balance between inhibition (holding back or not freely expressing yourself) and disinhibition ('letting it all hang out' or expressing yourself without any regard to others) may lead to least social difficulty. However, it's also true that having disinhibited people around can make for a good party while having inhibited people around can introduce a valuable sensitivity to others, as well as a note of caution that may be valuable.

Shyness and rudeness

It is clear that the fear of intruding and of giving offence, or of being rude, has something to do with shyness.

The difficulty of asking questions

Shy people often find it hard to ask questions. Why is this the case? Well, questions are extremely useful socially, but they also run the risk of appearing rude. One of the main ways in which people find out about each other is by asking questions, but the conventions about what is acceptable and what is not vary. In order to develop the manners and the sensitivity that fit with the culture you live in, you must be sensitive to these conventions.

There are many ways in which asking questions might be intrusive or offensive. They can be too personal, or a product of idle curiosity, or they can make someone feel that they are being interrogated. Some questions are clearly rude; for example: 'How did you get so rich?' 'Why is he so fat?'

During childhood we all learn a large number of social rules, for example about not interrupting, or talking too much about ourselves, or upsetting other people. We also learn that it is wrong, embarrassing and even unacceptable, to do these or similar things. Conventions vary, even between people who share the same background but are of different ages. So it is always possible to be rude by mistake.

The dangers of being rude

Why is it such a terrible thing to be rude? Tick the statements below that you feel apply to you:

☐ **1** In a social situation I'm terribly worried about upsetting people and about what they might think of me

☐ **2** I believe that being rude to someone is just about the worst thing you can do

☐ **3** To me, social life feels like finding my way through a minefield of potentially explosive devices – it all feels like a disaster waiting to happen

☐ **4** If I'm rude to someone (even if it's unintentional) other people are likely to reject me

☐ **5** If I'm rude to someone I've failed myself

☐ **6** As a child I was punished for being rude to people

If you ticked all or many of these statements it may be that you are overly concerned about being rude, especially by mistake. Such mistakes may have too much significance for you. We all make mistakes in social situations. In Part Three, Sections 1 and 2 you will find practical exercises to help you grow in confidence in all situations.

The problem with social rules

Knowing the rules about what is rude and what is not is certainly helpful. The problem is we all receive messages as children that are hard to fit together. For example we may be told 'Look at me when I'm talking to you' and 'Don't look at me like that'. Knowing the rules is never enough.

There are always exceptions, and they often have to be adapted to particular circumstances. Shyness makes people uncertain about how to adapt, and makes them feel too inhibited to attempt to do things differently. When this happens, misunderstandings can easily arise. For example, one person thinks, 'If he wanted me to know, then he would tell me,' and does not ask questions because of not wanting to intrude. But the other person thinks, 'She never asks, so she's not interested'. Both of them keep quiet when that is not what either of them really wants.

Do you find it difficult to ask relevant or important questions? Can you think of times when this has caused misunderstandings? Describe your experiences here.

_____

_____

_____

_____

_____

_____

_____

_____

_____

The minefield can be negotiated more easily by learning to be sensitive to other people. Picking up the signals, and repairing the damage when you have done something 'wrong', are important skills to learn. Unfortunately neither of these can be done so well when you are feeling self-conscious.

The self-awareness and self-focused attention of shy and socially anxious people may make them less aware of others and more at risk of giving offence by mistake. But at the same time, feeling shy or socially anxious makes it seem especially important not to be rude or to give offence. So shy and socially anxious people seem to be caught both ways. This workbook will give you practical strategies to overcome just this kind of problem.

Variations in different cultures

Shyness appears to occur everywhere in the world, but not to the same degree. Of course, no one has yet collected information about the forms of shyness present in every single country and culture in the world, but nevertheless some generalizations are starting to emerge. For example, among young adults shyness appears to affect only about one-third of the people in Israel but nearly two-thirds of those in Japan.

Within each culture it seems that shyness affects men and women equally. However, culturally there are differences in the ways in which people understand and react to shyness in men and in women.

It is generally considered to be a more feminine than masculine trait, and to be more acceptable in women than in men. Shy middle-aged women may remain shy but no longer find that this causes them any problems if they live a rather traditional, family-oriented life, focused on a local, well-known community. But shy men develop, and keep on using, more ways of concealing their shyness from others. They learn how to hide behind the 'rules of the game', or the structure required by their work or business situations, and to adopt the roles needed for the functions they perform without involving themselves personally.

People everywhere, and of both sexes, know that having a drink can make them feel less inhibited socially. Shy people as well as socially anxious ones use alcohol to help them feel better, in an attempt to boost their confidence. We look at some of the problems of using alcohol in this way in Part Two, page 9.

What does it all mean?

Clearly, shyness and social anxiety are close relatives and there is much overlap in their symptoms and in their effects. The strategies that have been shown to be helpful in overcoming social anxiety are also valuable for overcoming shyness.

In the rest of this book we'll use the term **social anxiety** instead of saying **social anxiety and shyness** each time. You can expect that the ideas you will read about apply to shyness as well as to social anxiety throughout. In particular, all the strategies for overcoming the problems will make sense whether you see your problem as mainly shyness or social anxiety.

Summary

1   Shyness is almost universal, although about half the people who suffer from it in childhood overcome the problem as adults.

2   The symptoms of shyness are similar to those of social anxiety.

3   Shyness is different from introversion. Introverted people have a less sociable style than extroverted ones, and shy people may be either introverts or extroverts.

4   The effects of shyness are wide-ranging, similar to those of social anxiety, and extend to all aspects of life, professional as well as personal.

5   Shyness has advantages as well as disadvantages, and can be an attractive characteristic. Our social life probably benefits from having the full range of people in it: shy or inhibited as well as bold or disinhibited.

6   Shy people often fear being rude, or giving offence, and are careful not to do this by mistake.

7   There are probably some cultural differences in shyness, but few differences between the frequency of the problem in men and in women.

8   The term social anxiety will be used from now on to refer to shyness as well.

SECTION 5: Is Social Anxiety All in the Mind? The Central Role of Thinking in Social Anxiety

This section will help you understand:

- How important the way you think is in social anxiety
- How social anxiety affects what you pay attention to
- What happens when you have negative automatic thoughts
- The effect of your underlying beliefs and assumptions
- The role of images in social anxiety
- How the meaning of social situations can start to change.

The way you think when you have social anxiety

Social anxiety is rooted in thoughts. Socially anxious people think that others think badly of them, or that they are judging them. This is why social situations seem so likely to lead to humiliation and embarrassment.

To make matters worse, socially anxious people think that the things that they suppose other people are thinking are true. You may think such things as:

- 'They don't want me with them.'
- 'They think I'm weird.'
- 'They don't like me.'

Underneath you may believe that you are different or odd and don't quite belong. Or you believe that you are certain to do something embarrassing or inept; to reveal your inadequacies or to be rejected, even if you have not put these beliefs into words. The fear, anxiety and distress of social anxiety are closely linked to such thoughts, and to the meaning that having such thoughts has.

So thinking plays a central part in social anxiety. Understanding this part of the problem is essential in working out exactly how to overcome it.

What you think affects what you feel

A major breakthrough in psychology over the past few decades has been a concept that at first may seem quite straightforward, even simple:

In most situations throughout our lives, what you think affects how you feel. It works the other way round too, so that how you feel affects what you think.

This is the main idea behind the development of cognitive behavioural therapy (CBT). It turns out, however, that the way this apparently simple principle works in practice is not so straightforward. We will show you next how this works in social anxiety.

Thinking can trigger bouts of anxiety ('I'm making a complete idiot of myself') and it can keep the anxiety going once it has started. Thinking 'I can't think of anything to say', or 'They're all going to judge me, and criticize me for being so idiotic', will only prolong the bad feelings, and influence how you behave when you are with other people.

In addition, the attitudes, beliefs and assumptions that people have can make them more or less vulnerable to social anxiety in the first place. You may believe such negative ideas as:

- 'I'm just not acceptable as I am.'

- 'Anybody I like wouldn't like me.'

- 'I'm different, or odd.'

So the many ways that you think contribute to the development and to the maintenance of your anxiety. If you could only change the way that you think, then you would be likely to change your feelings and your behaviour as well.

What do we mean by thinking?

Thoughts do not come like sentences, with capital letters at the beginning and full stops at the end. It is just that when we talk about them we usually express them in sentences.

Some thoughts are relatively easy to identify, for example:

- 'They're all looking at me.'

- 'I'm not doing this right.'

Some thoughts are much harder to identify, partly because you may feel they go without saying: for example, knowing that 'I'm just not up to it'.

Some of the things that we think – or that we know or remember – are extremely difficult to put into words. Thoughts include many processes, ideas and images that go on in your mind as well as straightforward thoughts. They include, for example:

- Attitudes, ideas and expectations

- Memories, impressions and images

- Beliefs and assumptions.

We have many words for referring to the contents of our minds. Some of these types of thoughts are obvious and easy to recognize, but others are harder. One way of making sense of the relationship between thoughts and feelings is to define differ-ent levels of thought processes. We can group them into three types of thinking:

1 The level of attention we pay to things. This determines what we notice.

2 The level of our automatic thoughts. These thoughts are going on all the time even without our realizing it. They reflect our spontaneous reactions to things.

3 What we believe and assume about ourselves and other people – these are called our **beliefs**.

Let's look at each of these types of thinking in turn.

The first way of thinking: the level of attention

First, social anxiety affects what you notice – what you pay attention to.

CASE STUDY: Judy

When Judy was talking to her boss, Michael, she suddenly felt hot and sweaty. She was sure she was going red, and wanted to hide her face. She noticed that he seemed rather distant, but was puzzled by this. She had not properly heard what he had said, and won-dered what she had done wrong.

CASE STUDY: Don

Don was listening to the banter going on between two workmates at the next bench. He noticed them glance his way, and felt himself withdrawing inside, seeking protection inside his 'shell'. He became preoccupied with the fear that they were going to say something to him. He felt too nervous and shaky to think of anything to say back to them, especially anything amusing or witty, and he was worried about what they thought about him for not being able to join in.

As soon as they became anxious, Judy and Don both noticed the things that went on inside them. Judy noticed her internal sensations of blushing while Don noticed his feeling of wanting to withdraw. They both found it difficult to engage with what was going on around them. Instead they focused their attention on their own concerns rather than those of the people with them. Once it was all over, it was easier to remember how bad and how foolish they felt than it was to remember exactly what anyone else had said or done.

These case studies show how social anxiety focuses people's attention on themselves. They also show how self-focused attention makes people feel increasingly self-conscious. When we are socially anxious we can become painfully aware of ourselves and of what we see as our shortcomings. It is difficult to forget the trembling hands or the glowing face once the trembling or blushing has begun. Once you start thinking about these symptoms they tend to dominate, so there is less attention left over for anything else.

In the case study above, Judy thought she must have missed something that her boss Michael had said. Don had no idea what his colleagues were really talking about when he noticed them glancing in his direction, or what they did next, once he had withdrawn into his shell. All he could remember was their tone of voice.

Looking out for danger

Both Judy and Don noticed the people around them first. They both tended to keep on the lookout for the types of situations that they found threatening, watching out for any dangers that they might be able to avoid.

Psychologists call this **hypervigilance** and it is part of a natural mechanism we all have for keeping safe. When we are being hypervigilant we direct our attention towards potential threats. The things that Judy and Don paid attention to were linked to their particular kind of fear: to their social anxiety. Judy felt socially inferior and inadequate, and was especially uncomfortable talking to people in authority over her. What she noticed was that Michael seemed rather distant, and this made her wonder what she might have done wrong. Don felt socially inept, and thought that other people found him too serious and slow-witted. What he noticed was the bantering tone of the conversation nearby, and the glance in his direction.

Describe a recent social situation you found difficult here. Can you remember how you felt? Can you remember what people actually said or did? What did you notice?

The situation:

_____

_____

_____

_____

How I felt:

_____

_____

_____

What other people said or did:

_____

_____

_____

_____

It's worth remembering...

What you pay attention to affects what gets into your mind. When you are socially anxious your attention is more self-focused, you are on the look-out for threats, and you notice and remember the things that fit with your fears.

Look again at the situation you described above. Did any of the things you noticed fit with your particular fears? Write down here what you fear most and what you noticed.

_____

_____

_____

The second way of thinking: the level of automatic thoughts

Everything that happens to us makes us think. Even though we might not be aware of doing so, we are thinking all the time. The things that we think reflect the ways in which we understand or interpret things that happen to us and around us.

- Sometimes our interpretation will be accurate.

- Sometimes our interpretation will be overoptimistic, as if we saw the world through rose-tinted spectacles.

- Sometimes our interpretation will be overpessimistic, as if we saw only the negative possibilities.

For example, when a stranger smiles at Don from the case study, he could think one of three things. He could think (accurately) that she is being friendly. He could think optimistically that she thinks he looks wonderful. Or he could think pessimistically that she could see he is feeling uncomfortable and is just trying to be kind.

When you are anxious you tend to look at things negatively more often than not. You tend to interpret things in terms of threats, as if the world were full of dangerous risks, and as if you are not able to deal with these risks. **Negative automatic thoughts** dominate your thinking. Tick any of the statements below that you often find yourself thinking in a social situation.

- [ ] I'll look foolish

- [ ] They think I'm ... stupid ... no good ... boring

- [ ] I'll lose control of myself, and my anxiety will show

- [ ] Everyone is looking at me

- [ ] I don't belong

☐ They can see how nervous I am

☐ I can't concentrate, or think straight

☐ Everything I say is nonsense

☐ This is terrible: a complete disaster

☐ They don't like me

☐ I'm always doing things wrong

These are all example of negative automatic thoughts. Later you will learn how to re-examine these automatic thoughts.

The third way of thinking: the level of underlying beliefs and assumptions

Your underlying beliefs reflect patterns of thinking and your assumptions reflect your major rules for living. They provide the building blocks for the attitudes you have about things.

Normally there is not much need for people to put their beliefs and assumptions into words. If you believe that most people are honest and trustworthy, then there is usually no need to say so unless you have a good reason to do so. This might happen if you were suddenly in doubt, or if you were asked specifically for your opinion.

For instance, think of someone you know quite well, like a colleague at work or a neighbour or friend. You probably have a general impression of what they're like as a person. Now imagine you had to write a reference for them. You would have to think about it in detail, and try to put your impressions into words. You would probably draw on many things that you know and could remember about that person's character, their behaviour, their way of talking to people, attitudes, history and so on.

But generally speaking we don't have to analyse our impressions and beliefs in that much detail. We don't have to check where they come from or why we think the way we do.

How we form our beliefs and assumptions

Our beliefs and assumptions about people are built up on a large body of information including:

● Our own experience

- What we observe

- What other people tell us

- How we feel about other people

- What we have learned

- What we can remember

- What we know about other people who seem like them

and much else besides.

Some of our beliefs will fit with people being honest and trustworthy, but some of it might not fit. Underlying beliefs and assumptions convey basic, and usually unspoken, attitudes and overall impressions, and they are often quite hard to phrase in precisely the way that feels right.

What exactly are your beliefs?

It can be very difficult to define your own beliefs. This is partly because it is easy to be swayed by fleeting impressions you might form at any one particular time.

However, trying to work out what your beliefs are is very important. Our beliefs and assumptions often provide the framework for how we see the world. They may also guide us in how we deal with the experiences that come our way.

It's worth remembering...

Our beliefs provide the colour of the glass in the spectacles through which we look out on the world. Our assumptions provide us with rules for living based on those beliefs.

So if you believe that people are basically fair-minded you might assume that 'if you treat people right they will do the same by you'. If you believe that other people are basically hostile or critical you might assume that 'if you reveal too much about your-self, then others will discover your weaknesses and exploit them'.

Read the statements opposite and tick any that reflect that way you think. If you think of other beliefs or assumptions you have about yourself, write them in the space provided. It may feel distressing to do this but it is very important to try to identify your negative beliefs when trying to overcome your anxiety problem. We'll be looking in more detail at negative beliefs, why they are unlikely to be true and how to replace them with more accurate, positive beliefs in Part Three, Section 2.

Beliefs:

I'm odd ☐   weird ☐   different ☐   boring ☐   stupid ☐   unattractive ☐

I'm inferior ☐   inadequate ☐   unacceptable ☐   unlikeable ☐

I can't change ☐   I'm stuck ☐   There's no hope for me ☐

Nobody I like would like me ☐

Others don't like people who are nervous ☐   anxious ☐   quiet ☐   shy ☐

People are always judging me ☐   criticizing ☐   looking out for things I do wrong ☐

There is a right way of doing things ☐

It is wrong to break social rules and conventions ☐

Other:

_____

_____

_____

_____

Assumptions:

☐ I must be amusing and interesting or people won't like me

☐ If I am alone I am bound to be unhappy

☐ You've got to do things right if you're going to be acceptable

☐ If others want to know me they'll let me know

☐ If the conversation doesn't go well it is my fault

☐ People will take advantage of me if I show signs of weakness

Other:

_____

_____

_____

_____

The beliefs and assumptions listed above are common in people with social anxiety. It's easy to see their negativity and to understand how they make you feel bad.

Beliefs

Some of the beliefs that we have listed are like variations on a theme. For example, the statement: 'Others don't like people who are ... nervous ... anxious ... quiet ... shy.' We have listed the belief like this because although people have similar beliefs, the precise way in which they describe them varies greatly from person to person.

Beliefs are statements about the way things 'are', or seem to be. They reflect opinions and attitudes about:

- **Yourself** (for example, 'I always do the wrong thing')

- **Other people** (for example, 'Other people always seem to know what to do')

- The way things are in **the world** in general ('terrible things can happen at the drop of a hat').

All three types of belief, about yourself, about other people and about the world, have a major impact on what you think, feel and do. They therefore also have a big impact on the ways in which you interact with the others around you. So they are an important factor when social anxiety becomes a problem.

Assumptions

Assumptions are like rules for living. They are closely related to the strategies that people use to cope with their social anxiety.

For example, if you assume that it is your fault when a conversation goes badly then you will try to make sure that none of the conversations you are involved in are bad ones. You might do this by:

- Avoiding as many conversations as possible

- Trying to say exactly the right thing

- Planning what to say in advance

- Making sure that you always let the other person take the lead without imposing your ideas

or in yet another way that will depend on you.

People with similar assumptions may adopt different strategies for dealing with the same type of problem. As we saw earlier, they also adopt different strategies for keeping themselves safe.

Later on, in Part Three, we will look at ways of re-examining your beliefs and assumptions and in turn changing the ways that you behave and feel.

Images in social anxiety

Another important way of thinking when we suffer from social anxiety is thinking in images. The tendency to think in images varies from person to person. Some people do not use imagery much, while others seem to use imagery all the time. They can bring to mind visual pictures of the things that happened to them almost as if they were turning on a video or DVD.

Sometimes these images are purely visual, but sometimes they include sounds, smells or tastes as well. It's as if all the senses help build the image in their mind. People may have this powerful visual thinking ability whether or not they suffer from social anxiety.

The power of images

Images are very powerful. They seem to describe an enormous amount of information in a very efficient way. The result of this is that they often provoke strong feelings. Images also come and go quickly – sometimes so quickly that people are not aware of having them until they stop and ask themselves, or stop and think about it.

Sometimes, when you suddenly notice a change in your feelings that you are unable to understand or to explain, thinking about whether you had any images may provide the explanation you were looking for.

CASE STUDY: Susan

Susan has suffered from social anxiety for many years. Recently she suddenly felt very nervous when asked a question by an older man at work. She could not understand why she had felt so nervous at the time. It was only later that she realized her nervousness was triggered by an image of herself in the past.

Susan remembered herself blushing in answer to an embarrassing personal question asked her by an uncle. This had happened at a family party when, in the hearing of many people, he had inquired teasingly about her relationship with someone he assumed (wrongly) was her boyfriend. When she denied there was anything special about the relationship, he continued to tease her. He implied that she was not telling the truth and was too embarrassed to admit to it.

Something that the two situations had in common appeared to have made the image pop into her mind again. With it came all the nervousness and embarrassment of that first situation.

It is common for images to be based, like Susan's, on specific memories. They may have a strong and immediate effect on the way you feel even if the memories are not clear and precise, but are more like overall impressions.

The impression of looking foolish in front of the class at school, or of being wrongly criticized and blamed for something, may leave behind a vivid image. The image may then come to mind in various situations later on, all of which are related in some way to the original situation.

For example, the same image, or impression, may come to mind in situations that produce the same sorts of feelings, or in situations where someone might speak in the same tone of voice, or say some of the same words, or look like the person who first provoked those feelings.

Do you have any powerful images in your mind of embarrassing or difficult events in your past like Susan's? Describe one of them here.

_____

_____

_____

_____

_____

_____

Ways of seeing

When you have images involving yourself, you can see yourself in the image in one of two ways.

1 You may be looking at the situation from the outside in, so to speak, as if you could see yourself from someone else's point of view.

2 You may look at the situation from the inside out, as if you were looking at the situation in which you find yourself through your own eyes.

Seeing things from the inside, looking outwards, focuses attention on other people. In this way you can observe and gather accurate information about them: about their feelings and reactions, about whether they were listening, paying attention, interested in what was happening and so on.

Socially anxious people are more likely than other people to say they see things from the outside in. In their images they often see themselves as they assume others would see them. If they feel hot and bothered, then in their images they see themselves as looking hot and bothered (even if in reality their feelings were totally invisible to others).

The effects of seeing things from the outside in

Seeing things this way has a number of effects.

1 It tends to make you feel worse. You become increasingly aware of the way you feel, and how that must look to others.

2 Becoming more aware of your appearance, even if you are quite wrong about it, makes you feel more self-conscious.

3 Being preoccupied with yourself makes it hard to pay attention to others, and to be sure about what is really going on, or what it means.

4 The image reflects what the you fear rather than reality. If you fear looking stupid, then that is the way you see yourself in the image. As images are such efficient ways of conveying meaning, the image has an immediate impact, even if it is only fleeting. If you see yourself looking stupid, you might think this means that everyone can spot your weaknesses right away, and that this is proof that you are basically socially inadequate.

In this way, images seem to confirm your underlying beliefs, even though in reality this is not the case. These images can only reflect and reveal your beliefs.

This kind of socially anxious imagery helps to explain the symptoms of social anxiety. It also explains one of the ways in which they can suddenly increase.

To overcome social anxiety it helps to learn how to consciously control imagery, and how to explore ways of taking a different perspective. This could involve, for example, searching for images and memories of competent and effective interactions you've had with people to replace powerful negative images and memories. You could also make a conscious effort to try to see situations the other way round, from the inside out. In that way you can pay better attention to other people and the details of the social event in question.

The meaning of social situations

We've seen from the examples above that the mind makes links between events with similar meanings, and that images may convey these meanings most efficiently. We generate images in our own minds after all and the power that generates them, and influences the form that they take, once again is our mind.

We form images based on particular beliefs and assumptions, and images reflect these beliefs in pictures or in words, or in other more symbolic ways, as in dreams.

For example, having a fleeting image of a moment when you floundered for words, and everything you said seemed to be muddled and confused, may carry with it various meanings. These could include:

- 'I always make myself look stupid'.

- 'I'm no good at talking to people'.

- 'No one would want much to do with me'.

Indeed, often it is the meaning something has that is the most important part of it, and produces the strongest feelings.

When your social anxiety starts to change, then meanings change also. As your confidence grows, then a setback or disappointment (such as someone being unable to come with you to the cinema) no longer has its original meaning, for example about being rejected, and about not being acceptable to others. Instead of being stuck in seeing the refusal as a personal rejection, it becomes possible to step outside this framework, and to start thinking differently: trying out new 'meanings', such as

'Maybe they were busy', 'Perhaps I need to meet more people'. This course will help you learn to change the meaning of these events to you.

Summary

1   Thinking plays a central role in social anxiety.

2   What you think affects how you feel. This is the basis for cognitive behavioural therapy.

3   There are many kinds of thinking, and thoughts are not always easy to put into words.

It is useful to distinguish three levels of thinking:

- **Attention**: what you notice and pay attention to: socially anxious people notice things that fit with their fears

- **Negative automatic thoughts**: these are like the stream of consciousness in your head, or the internal conversation you have with yourself or with others

- **Beliefs and assumptions**: underlying beliefs and assumptions about yourself, about other people and about the world are all likely to be relevant.

4   Imagery can play an important, unrecognized part in social anxiety. Images are often fleeting, but they trigger strong feelings and reflect underlying meanings.

5   As social anxiety changes, the meaning of social difficulties also changes. Once their significance is less devastating they will have a less distressing effect on you.

SECTION 6: Where Does Social Anxiety Come From? What Causes It?

This section will help you understand:

- The role played by your biological or genetic makeup in social anxiety

- The effect of the environment in which you grew up

- The effect of bad experiences

- The demands of different stages in your life

- The effect of everyday stresses.

CASE STUDY: Jim

Jim was sitting with a group of people during a break in the working day. They were talking light-heartedly about the new procedures for booking annual leave. During a brief lull in the conversation someone asked him: 'How do you think the changes will affect you?'

Jim's mind went blank. He could not think of anything to say. He thought that everyone was looking at him, and the silence that followed seemed to go on forever, while he stared at the floor.

Finally he managed to mumble, 'I don't really know,' and the conversation continued around him while he felt mortified: stupid, embarrassed, and angry with himself for not being able to answer such a simple question more easily. He was sure that he had just confirmed their general impression of him as totally inadequate.

What was the cause of Jim's anxiety? The first answer to this question is: 'other people'. Someone asked Jim a question, all the people in the group were looking at him as he tried to answer it, and for Jim other people are the cause of his problem. The question he was asked made his mind go blank, and triggered a set of events that he found extremely embarrassing. He ended up feeling stupid and angry with himself as well as anxious, and found the whole event undermining and humiliating. If no one had asked him a question it would never have happened.

There is obviously more to the problem than the fact that someone asked Jim a question. The immediate cause of his anxiety is only one of many factors.

Causes are always complex. There are many factors that contribute to social anxiety, and they do this in different ways. Different things will be important for different people.

The first factor we will look at is whether you are 'born' to be socially anxious. What role does your biological makeup play?

Biological factors: what you are born with

Some anxiety factors are shared by everyone. For example, it seems to be part of everyone's biological makeup to feel nervous or threatened by eyes. People with social anxiety often avoid making eye contact without realizing that, for everyone, looking someone in the eye releases nervous energy.

Looking someone in the eye stimulates our nervous system. This makes it hard to hold eye contact for long without blinking or looking away. Being stared at makes most people feel uncomfortable so that they feel 'stared down', and then look away. Interestingly, eye contact can also be threatening to animals. Staring at an aggressive animal can hold the attacker at bay and the eye spots on the wings of a butterfly, flashed at the right moment, can put potential predators off their stride (or strike).

There are some biological factors associated with stress and threat that we all have in common, and some that vary between individuals. Two of these varying factors can play a part in the development of social anxiety. They are:

1 The speed and intensity with which someone's nervous system responds when it is stimulated

2 Your personality or temperament.

The arousal system

Our nervous system is designed to help us survive. When we feel threatened stress hormones such as adrenaline are released throughout the body. These hormones have a number of direct effects on the body such as:

- Increasing our heart rate

- Causing us to sweat

- Changes in the digestive system

- A heightening of our senses.

These effects prepare us either for a fight or to run away from a dangerous situation.

Researchers have found that some people's nervous systems respond much more quickly and intensively to any kind of threat. These people are described as having a **highly reactive arousal system**.

If you have a highly reactive arousal system you will be likely to notice physical changes such as an increase in your heart rate, or in the amount that you sweat, sooner and more intensely than someone whose system is less reactive.

A good thing or a bad thing?

It is not necessarily a bad thing to be highly reactive. You could see it as a kind of sensitivity to people and experiences. It could be an asset to be used both in personal and in social situations. For example, it could make you very aware of and sensitive to people's moods and the general atmosphere.

However, many people see being highly reactive as a negative thing – they see it as a tendency to over-react and a sign of being hypersensitive.

It's worth remembering…

Having an easily aroused nervous system doesn't have to be a handicap. It depends how you look at it and how you manage your reaction.

Intense levels of arousal and of anxiety are uncomfortable for everyone. Everyone can have them, and people adapt to the system they are born with. We know that anxiety can run in families, and this suggests that the genes you inherit from your parents could be a factor in your social anxiety. However, although people with anxious parents are statistically more likely than others to suffer from anxiety, the kind of anxiety that troubles them may be different from the one that troubled either of their parents.

Causes of social anxiety: some contributory factors

Biological factors: what you are born with, e.g.:

- An arousal system that responds quickly, is easily triggered into intense reactions
- Temperament: being more or less sociable, extrovert, shy

Environmental factors: what happens to you, e.g.:

- Relationships with parents and with the people who cared for you in childhood
- Your experience of being evaluated, criticized, praised, appreciated, etc.
- Opportunities for social learning, making friendships, intimacy, etc.
- The ways in which you learned to cope, e.g. by facing up to things or by avoiding them

Bad and traumatic experiences, e.g.:

- Being bullied, victimized, left out, teased or tormented; being rejected
- Having to cope without sufficient support, e.g. if parents were ill or absent, or died

Difficulties coping with demands of different life stages, e.g.:

- Childhood: learning to interact with other people; stages of shyness
- Adolescence: defining an identity, becoming independent, discovering sexuality
- Maturity: balancing self-reliance and dependence, control and submission; belonging
- Retirement: loss of the working role, or of colleagues

Stresses that affect relationships with others, e.g.:

- Major moves: new home; friends or family moving away
- Important changes: a first baby; having to work in a group; managing others
- Competition: thinking that if you are not a winner, then you must be a loser

Other people are not the cause of the problem. The things they do can trigger the symptoms.

Temperament or personality

People also vary in their temperament or personality. Newborn babies are strikingly different right from the start – even if only their parents know it. Some are calm and others more excitable; some seem sociable and others less so.

As they develop, some babies remain happier than others when on their own, and ready to entertain themselves, while others appear to prefer company. All babies are relatively calm around strangers at first, and they are not distressed by being handed round from person to person. Later they go through a stage of being shy and more wary of being with people they do not already know, and easily become distressed if separated from familiar people. But the degree to which strangers upset them varies enormously.

Of course, biological differences between people are not the only factor determining how a child responds to new people, even in the first year of life. Babies are constantly learning from and responding to the reactions of those around them. Babies may:

- Pick up signs of anxiety from their parents

- Their parents may not be able to comfort and reassure them when they are distressed

- The strangers they meet may be insensitive to the needs of small babies and do alarming things.

Nevertheless, temperamental differences between babies exist, and they may help to create the conditions in which social anxiety can subsequently develop.

Biology isn't everything

Biological differences are unlikely to be the whole cause of the problem. Also their effects can be changed by what happens later in your life. Having a sensitive arousal system, or a less outgoing temperament, does not necessarily lead to social anxiety. In the same way being born with relatively long legs and an aptitude for sport might not make someone into a good runner. It might do so, but there will be many people with long legs and an aptitude for sport who are not particularly good at – or interested in – running. Similarly, there are many supersensitive people with unsociable (or introverted) personalities who are not socially anxious.

Socially anxious people often think that things would be different if only they were different in some way: better-looking, thinner, more intelligent or funnier, more interesting or sexually attractive, more creative or imaginative. You may assume that you are handicapped by being born the way you are; that there is nothing you can do to change it.

But this is not the case.

It's worth remembering...

People of all kinds, whatever their assets or apparent handicaps, can make friends, find partners, enjoy relationships with others and feel socially confident.

Even more surprisingly to some, highly attractive, good-looking, intelligent and successful people can suffer from high levels of social anxiety. Other factors, including environmental ones, also contribute to the problem.

The environment: what happens to you

Social relationships are first made at home, and this goes for relationships with people in the family as well as with people outside it. In their families people learn important social lessons such as:

- What is acceptable or not acceptable in terms of behaviour

- What it means to feel loved and to feel unloved

- Being accepted for what you are, or being rejected.

We all learn these lessons as we grow up, and our experience provides the background to our beliefs and assumptions about what other people think of us. Being liked, loved and accepted by others, friends as well as family, conveys a sense of your own personal value and self-worth. It provides the setting and conditions for building self-esteem and for feeling confident with other people.

The message you carry away

Of course things are not always perfect. Everyone as they are growing up does some things that other people object to such as telling lies, saying cruel or unkind things to others, or setting out to hurt somebody else. Children are likely to be punished for such behaviour. In addition no parent, teacher or other adult is ever perfectly fair, and always in touch with the needs of a particular child, so all children are likely to feel they've been treated unreasonably from time to time.

However, family life does not have to be perfect for people to feel socially confident. If the overall message a person grows up with helps them to feel that they are accepted and 'belong', if it helps them to relate to others in ways that they wish to, some mishaps need not matter and do not cause problems.

What if the message wasn't positive

If the overall message is not positive or helpful – if it is definitely negative, or if it leaves room for doubt – then some people become uncertain about their ability to relate to others. They are uncertain about their acceptability or adequacy or lovability, and about the ways in which people will react to them. Anxiety is built upon uncertainty.

It is harder to become socially confident if you never know whether you will be praised or criticized, when you will get yelled at, or told to get lost. Your confidence can also be undermined if there is no one more consistent to turn to for support. Such experiences may produce deep-seated problems.

On the other hand these experiences may cause few or only temporary difficulties, for example if it happens at home but not at school, or in one class but not in the next one. Having one staunch supporter, or one person who understands, can make all the difference.

What was your home or school environment like? Was it generally positive or negative? Describe your experiences here.

_____

_____

_____

_____

_____

How we feel we've been judged

On page 52 we learnt how socially anxious people tend to think that other people pass judgement on them. They assume that they are being evaluated and that the evaluation will reveal that they fail to come up to the mark.

People are not born with such ideas ready in their heads. Our best guess as to where these ideas come from is that they are a product of what happens in a person's childhood and adolescence.

The ways in which we are evaluated as we grow up, for better and for worse, tell us about what is acceptable in our social world, and about what is not. They can help us to behave in socially acceptable ways, and help us to build the confidence that mistakes can be put right. We can learn that if we are rejected this will only be temporary and in any case we are not being completely rejected. Unfortunately the opposite can also happen.

People may feel rejected, inadequate or unacceptable if:

- The judgements they received were too harsh, too wide-ranging or constant

- Or if they were applied indiscriminately, regardless of what actually happened.

People may come to fear that their actions will reveal underlying weaknesses, or fundamental sources of badness, even if no such things exist. Then they may fear doing anything that could reveal what they see as their inadequacy or inferiority to others. Joining in a conversation may be enough to trigger such a sense of vulnerability, if it has been an important, dominant part of your early experience.

The meaning of the messages

In Section 5 (page 51) we listed some of the more distressing messages – or meanings – that people with social anxiety have ended up with as adults. It is possible that these messages were based on childhood experiences. People learn from experience such things as 'You've got to do things right to be acceptable', or 'I'm different from others, and odd'.

The bad news about these messages is that they can be deeply ingrained. They 'go without saying', in the way that someone just 'knows' they are not as good as others and never even questions this assumption.

But the good news is that the messages can be updated. You have learned them while you were growing up, and they are much more likely to be products of the ways in which you were treated than of any actual failings or weaknesses in you. You can unlearn these messages just as you learnt them.

When working with social anxiety it is easy to focus on the factors that contribute to causing the problem. You may forget about the positive things in your life, as if they were not relevant. When you think about the messages that you have picked up during your early experience, it is important to think about the positive as well as the negative messages. Try to keep the overall picture in perspective.

Everyone learns positive as well as negative things about themselves as they grow up, for example about their sensitivity, or humour, or kindness, or wish to be friendly. When the negative ones cause problems they tend to dominate your thinking.

Take time now to list some of the good and positive experiences you had with other people as a child.

_____

_____

_____

_____

_____

It's worth remembering...

Positive characteristics and positive messages that other people gave you as a child can easily be forgotten or denied when things go wrong, or when you're feeling bad. But discounting them is more likely to be an effect of feeling anxious and bad about yourself than a true reflection of what people think of you.

The need for appropriate opportunities

Another factor in the development of social anxiety is not getting enough experience in communicating and interacting with other people. Let's look at that more closely now.

Social worlds differ enormously from place to place, and the ways in which our parents talked to their friends and to each other are very different from the ways we now use and feel comfortable with. That goes for talking about ordinary things like making an arrangement to do something together, as well as for talking about things that we know people now think quite differently about, such as personal feelings or sex.

All of the little niceties about how things are done have to be learned, and none of them can be learned without real-life experience. For example, Rowena is 38, suffers from social anxiety and is recently single once more following her marriage breakdown. She has not been to a night club for years, and no longer knows how to behave in one. She has been to a number of formal work dinners, and feels confident enough to work out pretty quickly what will be required of her at the next one. She is not bothered by the possibility of putting a foot wrong in that situation, and knows she can ask if she is uncertain about something. Her lack of recent experiences in nightclubs is a problem, however, now that she is single again and wants to go out and socialize.

Not having the opportunity to learn how things are done can put you at a disadvantage. You need such opportunities as:

- Mixing with people of your own age

- Finding and making friends with like-minded people

- Being listened to

- Confiding in someone and sharing confidences

- Learning to talk about yourself

- Discovering what makes other people tick.

Lack of the relevant experience can contribute to social anxiety; and gathering relevant experience can help to solve the problem. For a person who wants to meet people, learning about night clubs could be much more useful – and much more fun – than learning how to handle formal work dinners. But it cannot be done without going and learning what to do.

The rules of the game

In some situations the rules of the game, so to speak, are clearer than in others. For example there are standard, conventional ways of:

- Ordering a meal in a restaurant

- Introducing one person to another

- Conducting a business meeting

- Chairing a committee

- Making requests or saying 'no' to unreasonable requests.

In many languages there are different forms of speech for talking to people, which vary according to how well you know them or how formal you want to be. In all of these cases, the only way to 'do it right' is to learn the rules, and it can be comforting to feel that there is a rule book to turn to in case of difficulty.

When there's no rule book

The problem is that, mostly, there is no rule book. There is nowhere you can look all the rules up; and even if there were, no one learns them all at once. So adults cannot usually approach unfamiliar situations with a complete set of social rules, ready to draw on whenever needed.

We all have to learn new rules for the new situations we find ourselves in as we do different and new things. Learning the rules usually involves a process of guesswork, whether you are joining a club or talking to your bank manager. Sometimes you get it right, and sometimes you get it wrong.

You can watch other people to see what they do, and you can ask. When it comes to trying it out for yourself you are bound to stumble at first, and produce a more awkward and less polished performance to begin with than you will later on. But just because you haven't had the chance to learn the rules doesn't mean you're always going to be at a disadvantage, socially.

We know that socially anxious people do as well as others in social situations when they are not anxious. The problem is not in your basic social abilities so much as in the fact that being anxious makes it hard to take full advantage of these abilities and to feel confident about using them.

Learning from the experience of problems

The way you have learned to cope with the problems you encounter and to deal with feeling anxious can also contribute to the development of social anxiety. Handling problems and anxiety is something that all of us learn, partly through practice and partly by watching the people around us and using them as models.

We know that facing problems works better in the long run than avoiding them – or drowning your sorrows in drink. You have a better chance of coping when you feel anxious if you:

- Learn to hang in there

- Are not too dismayed when things do not go your way

- Don't blame yourself too much for setbacks or difficulties.

What is not helpful is focusing on how to escape or avoid the situation, or on how to ensure that your vulnerabilities are well hidden from view. Wanting to avoid or keep safe tends to keep the problem going. Thinking this way contains the hidden message that facing the situation would be dangerous or risky.

Bad or traumatic experiences

Traumatic experiences cause extreme distress at the time that they occur, and they also leave their mark. They are hard to get over. Some of the most common ones reported by socially anxious people are experiences that happened at school.

Being bullied is one of these distressing experiences and the effects of being bullied are looked at in detail in Part Three, Section 5. However, you may also have been singled out or made to feel different and unacceptable by being teased for something that you could do nothing about, like having freckles or big ears or acne, or for being overweight.

When you are constantly treated like this it can feel like downright cruelty and victimization. The message you receive is a painful one: 'we don't want you', or 'you don't belong'.

Surprisingly, perhaps, being singled out seems to be part of the problem, as it can sometimes have a bad effect even when it happens for supposedly positive reasons. For example, being someone's favourite, at home or at school, can make you liable to be picked on by those who are less favoured, or it can make you feel like a misfit and different from others.

Were you bullied or singled out for being different at home or at school? Write about your experiences here.

_____

_____

_____

_____

_____

_____

In Part Three, Section 5 you will find practical strategies to help you overcome the legacy of bullying.

Why don't bad experiences make everyone socially anxious?

Being rejected for yourself is always a deeply distressing experience, and it can certainly lead to social anxiety. However, not all people who have been rejected or suffered through bad experiences become socially anxious. The reasons for this are not entirely clear.

Having a bad experience is only one of many things that happen to someone, and only one of many possible things that could make that person socially anxious. When bad experiences happen to someone, he or she may have been helped in a way that 'made the difference'. They may:

● Have been rescued by particular supporters, family members or friendships

● Have developed their own interests, skills or talents, which helped them to build their self-confidence and to keep their self-respect in difficult circumstances.

When you've had to grow up too fast

Anything that singles someone out as different, unacceptable, odd or weird in the judgement of others (and their judgements may be completely wrong, of course) can make a person more likely to suffer from social anxiety.

If you had to assume responsibilities beyond your years because your parents or the people caring for you were absent or had their own difficulties to deal with, you may have been too tired, worried or busy to have been able to take part in the social life going on around you. You may have had to grow up so quickly in some ways that you became out of touch with people your own age, and your real contemporaries may have seemed somewhat childish.

It is difficult to play, to relax or to talk freely about the things that are happening to you when you are extremely distressed, worried or over burdened as a child. So the experience sets you apart at the time, and crossing the gap later can be difficult and create anxieties.

Did you have to take on extra responsibilities as a child that set you apart from others? Write about your experiences here.

The demands of different life stages

Most people with social anxiety report that it began for them in one of two ways. Either they say:

1 They have always had social anxiety, that they have been nervous when meeting new people all their lives. They may describe themselves as being different, odd or inherently shy people.

2 They say that it became a problem in their teens and early twenties.

The challenges of adolescence

Adolescents and young people have to find their way around a large number of potential social stumbling blocks as they become increasingly independent of their families, seek out partners with whom to share their lives, and establish themselves in the adult roles that our society expects.

Handling all of these changes successfully is no easy task. Any social difficulties that you have had earlier in life may now re-emerge when things do not go right. These could include:

- The person you find most attractive opting for someone else

- Moving to a new place and finding your shyness makes it hard to make new friends

- When the only way you have learned to assert yourself is by being aggressive.

Did social anxiety become a problem for you during adolescence or your twenties? Describe how your difficulties started here.

_____

_____

_____

_____

_____

_____

Problems in later life

Patterns that you developed earlier in your life may make some later problems harder to deal with too. If you have always depended on having a crowd around you, at home, at school and at work, you will be especially prone to feeling isolated (and rejected) when:

- You leave school and start to work or go to college
- Your children leave home
- Your work requires you to move to a new place
- You retire and lose contact with colleagues.

All these changes can undermine your social confidence, and make it (temporarily at least) hard for you to become established in a new social context.

Has your social situation changed in any of these ways recently? Describe what has happened and how it may have affected you here.

_____

_____

_____

_____

Each stage of life presents its own set of social challenges, so a bout of social anxiety can arise at any stage in life.

Present stresses

Two kinds of stresses are especially likely to contribute to you feeling anxious. If your fears focus on your sense of what other people think about you, the anxiety is likely to take a social form. These two stresses are:

- Major moves which sever important social contacts with friends, family or colleagues, and

- Important changes that affect your ways of relating to other people.

These events are stressful because they demand adaptation. That takes energy at a time when you may have little to spare, and when your confidence has yet to be built up. Then old vulnerabilities may re-emerge.

Someone who has just been promoted may have to respond to many new demands, but may also have to start giving orders to people who were only recently friends on an equal footing. They may also have to present progress reports and future plans at meetings with 'important' people, whose judgements and criticisms may be made publicly.

Working women who have just had their first baby often go through a stage of feeling unconfident – about many things. When they are also stressed and relatively isolated, it is easy to find it additionally stressful to meet new and apparently more confident people. For them, the re-entry into the workplace later on can also bring on a similar, unconfident phase.

Have any of these major life changes happened to you recently? Have they affected your confidence? Describe your experiences here.

_____

_____

_____

_____

_____

_____

_____

How do all these factors interact?

When a problem has many potential causes it is hard to disentangle them. We'll look at this in more detail in the next section.

One simple way of thinking about causes of social anxiety is shown in the box below. This divides the main causes into **vulnerability factors** on the one hand and **stresses** on the other.

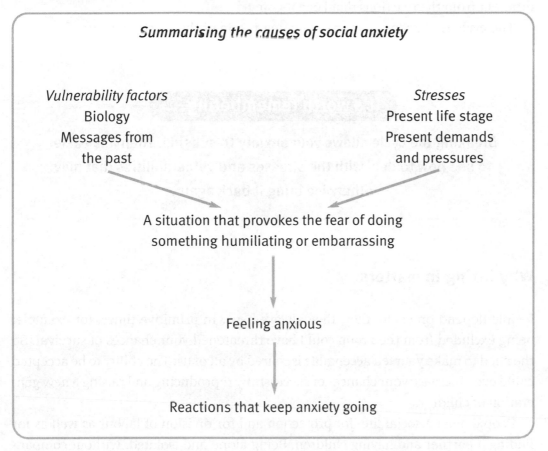

Summarising the causes of social anxiety

Vulnerability factors
Biology
Messages from
the past

Stresses
Present life stage
Present demands
and pressures

A situation that provokes the fear of doing
something humiliating or embarrassing

Feeling anxious

Reactions that keep anxiety going

Vulnerability factors are long-standing characteristics that make you more likely to suffer from bouts of social anxiety. They can be both biological and psychological.

Psychological vulnerability factors are the messages that we learn from the things that happened earlier in our life – from experience.

Stresses include the demands of your particular stage of life and any specific stressful factors or circumstances that are affecting you at the present time. These may be **internal pressures**, such as the desire to succeed, the need to be liked, or the fear of being alone. They can also be **external pressures**. What counts as a stress varies from person to person.

The diagram shows that if you have social anxiety, the problem will occur when you encounter situations that provoke the fear of doing something that will be humiliating or embarrassing. Once you feel anxious then a vicious cycle comes into play, and keeps the problem going.

Reactions to anxiety, such as looking for a way out, worrying about what others might notice, feeling self-conscious or finding it difficult to speak fluently, feed back to make the anxiety worse. So whatever caused the anxiety in the first place may be different from the reactions that keep it going.

The cycle that keeps your anxiety going is one of the most important factors to deal with when it comes to overcoming anxiety.

> ### It's worth remembering...
>
> Breaking the cycle allows your anxiety to subside. Then it is easier to see how to deal with the stresses and vulnerabilities that may otherwise bring it back again.

Why fitting in matters

People depend on each other; they always have. In primitive times, for example, being excluded from the group could have threatened your chances of survival. So the need to make yourself acceptable is shared by all of us. The ability to be accepted could even increase your chances of successfully reproducing and raising a new generation of children.

People need a social life, for protection and for division of labour as well as for finding a partner and having children. Being alone and isolated, without companions, is threatening, and hard to tolerate for long. It makes us feel vulnerable. It is no wonder that isolation is used as a form of punishment, or that hostility and rejection are alarming experiences to deal with.

It takes a huge amount of discipline and self-denial to live as a hermit, partly because having social support available provides a degree of protection. When bad things happen, those people who have support from others around them fare better than those who do not – which is not to say that social life does not have its own difficulties and dangers too.

Jim's story

These difficulties and dangers were all too apparent to Jim, whose inability to answer the question he was asked introduced this section (see page 67). He became tongue-tied and anxious when asked how the new arrangements for taking holidays from work were going to affect him.

If other people were not the cause of the problem for Jim, then what was? We know nothing about how vulnerable Jim's personality made him to social anxiety. Nor do we know about any stresses, demands or pressures on him. All that we do know is the reflection of these things in his mind (or the 'surface' problem).

The surface problem dominates Jim's experience, leaving him as well as us asking the question 'Why?' First his mind went blank, as he could not think of anything to say. Then he thought that everyone was looking at him, and became aware of the long silence that followed. After speaking he was so preoccupied with his feelings – mortified, embarrassed, angry – that he could no longer follow the conversation, and he ended up angry with himself. He was certain that he had, yet again, made a bad impression, and that everyone there thought of him as inadequate.

The way Jim's mind works when he is anxious provides the clues for understanding what to do about the problem. We do not have to know everything about all the factors that could have caused his social anxiety to understand how it could be reduced. Jim's thoughts are central, and they reflect the many processes that are set in motion when someone else's actions trigger his symptoms of anxiety.

How to understand these socially anxious patterns of thinking and how to start changing them will be explained in the next section.

Summary

1   Other people are not the main cause of social anxiety. Many other factors contribute to it.

2   These include both biological factors and environmental ones.

3   Experience of relationships as we grow up provides the framework for our thinking about how we relate to others, and bad experiences can leave long-lasting impressions.

4   Social life presents different demands at different stages.

5   Vulnerability factors and stresses combine to make someone more likely to suffer from social anxiety, and a vicious cycle operates to keep the anxiety going.

6   It is not necessary to know everything about what caused the problem in order to work out what to do to address it.

SECTION 7: Explaining Social Anxiety: Understanding What Happens When Someone Is Socially Anxious

This section will help you understand:

- What keeps social anxiety going

- How being self-conscious affects social anxiety

- How your beliefs and assumptions affect social anxiety

- What safety behaviours are and why they're a problem

- How expectations can make things worse

- The danger of over-analysing an event.

A new theory about social anxiety

In 1995 a new theory or model of social anxiety was published. The people who wrote it were two clinical psychologists who were researchers as well as practising therapists, David Clark and Adrian Wells. In this section we're going to look at their model in detail because:

- It helps us to understand what happens when someone suffering from social anxiety encounters one of the situations that makes them feel anxious

- It explains the vicious cycles that keep the problem going

- It suggests how social anxiety can be treated.

Many of the suggestions about how to solve the problem in Part Two of this course are based on this model.

This new model has many advantages over earlier theories:

- It is being backed up by careful research that so far has supported the ideas behind it

- It is consistent with some of the earlier theories about social anxiety, but also explains more clearly what should be done to overcome the problem

- It recognizes the central part played by thinking in social anxiety.

Although many people have found this model very helpful, remember no theory is ever fixed and no one has the one and only right and complete answer. The model will probably change and evolve in time but right now it has proven to be very useful.

Here are the main ideas behind the Clark and Wells model:

1 Social anxiety can be understood and explained. It is not a mysterious thing that will always be confusing and puzzling.

2 The way in which we understand social anxiety plays an essential part in understanding what to do about it.

3 The model is based on research by experienced clinicians and has been developed out of earlier models and theories. It is likely to benefit most people who suffer from social anxiety.

This model may not fit everyone exactly. But many people with social anxiety have found this theory very helpful and it may well work for you too.

The current model of social anxiety

A diagram of the model is shown opposite. Let's look at it in detail, starting from the top.

1 The trigger situation

Stage 1 of the model shows that a bout of social anxiety occurs when something triggers it off. We already know that the type of situation that triggers a bout of social anxiety varies from person to person.

For many people, for example, social anxiety is triggered by having to speak in front of a group of people.

2 Beliefs and assumptions

The diagram shows that when one of these situations occurs it activates your particular beliefs and assumptions. For example, when you have to speak in front of other people you may believe that they are being critical or making negative judgments about you.

3 You see the situation as dangerous

As a result, you see the situation as threatening and you interpret it as socially dangerous. This gives rise to thoughts such as:

- 'I'm going to do something wrong here.'

- 'I can't come over well, in the way that other people can.'

Thoughts like this cause distress and anxiety.

These patterns of thinking are central to the whole process of feeling socially anxious.

The Clark and Wells model of social anxiety

Trigger situation

Activates beliefs and assumptions

The situation is seen as being 'socially dangerous'

Self-consciousness
Attention focused on self

Safety behaviours

Signs and symptoms of anxiety

4 Self-consciousness

When socially anxious people get distressed they focus in on themselves. They become increasingly self-aware or self-conscious (this is shown in the circled part of the diagram).

Let's look at how this works in our example. If you have to speak in public and start to feel distressed you shift your attention inwards, on to the signs of social anxiety and social ineptitude of which you are painfully aware. You become more aware of the sound of your voice or the fact that you are blushing. You think that other people notice these things and this makes you increasingly conscious of yourself and of the way in which you think you are coming over to others.

In technical terms this is described as processing yourself as a social object. It's almost as if you are able to see yourself from the outside, as an observer would.

Your image of yourself

Of course we can't actually see ourselves as others see us. But that is how it seems to socially anxious people in their mind's eye.

As we saw in Section 5 (page 51), many socially anxious people have images of themselves when they feel anxious that fit with how they think – or fear – other people see them. They describe images of themselves doing things that to them are 'unacceptable', like blushing or trembling or stuttering. They describe their view of themselves in these images from 'outside in', as if they were able to see themselves as someone else would.

A vicious cycle

The more we focus on our own internal sensations and what we see as our shortcomings, the more self-conscious we become, and the more threatening, dangerous or risky the situations seem. This is why the arrows between the self-awareness circle in the diagram and the perceived social danger above it go in both directions. Focusing inwards makes people more aware of internal signs and sensations of social anxiety, and being aware of these experiences makes the situations seem more socially threatening.

Ways of thinking that don't help

This diagram reveals three particular ways of thinking that can keep social anxiety going. We first looked at these in Section 5, page 52.

What you notice or pay attention to

We've already seen how socially anxious people pay close attention to how they think they are doing, and pay less attention than other people do to others (see page 63). In the self-awareness cycle you can't help noticing yourself and how you think you are behaving; for example you notice that everyone is looking at you, and can't get that out of your mind.

Negative automatic thoughts

We first met negative automatic thoughts on page 56. You might like to re-read this section to remind yourself of what they are. In the diagram we can see how they are involved in seeing and interpreting social situations as threatening or dangerous. For example an obvious negative automatic thought when having to speak in front of people is: 'I'm not going to be able to think of anything to say'.

Underlying beliefs and assumptions

We looked at these on page 60. In the diagram we can see these are activated by the particular situations in question. For example, feeling anxious and incompetent when speaking in front of people can activate the underlying belief that 'I'm different. I don't really belong'.

These three types of thinking are central to the Clark and Wells theory. And they are central to the problem of social anxiety.

Let's now return to the diagram on page 89.

5 Safety behaviours and signs and symptoms of anxiety

There are two other consequences of seeing a situation as socially dangerous: safety behaviours and the signs and symptoms of anxiety. These are shown in the bottom corners of the diagram.

Safety behaviours

We first looked at safety behaviours on page 15. You might want to take a quick look at this section again and remind yourself of the safety behaviours you use.

It is only natural to keep yourself safe when you feel anxious or frightened. The ways you might do this could include only talking to 'safe' people, or about 'safe' topics; by hiding your 'real' self, or by not making eye contact. There are many ways of keeping safe. But whether or not they succeed, they lead you to the conclusion that without them things might have been even worse.

For example, you might think that if you had not kept a tight hold on yourself everyone would have seen your shaking, and thought the worse of you for it. Or you might think if you had spoken up and said what you felt instead of keeping quiet, you might have revealed some unacceptable things about yourself and turned people away from you.

Feeling at risk makes you want to keep safe, but trying to keep safe keeps you thinking that the situation is risky. One thing feeds into another to keep the problem going. A list of common safety behaviours is shown on page 16. We look at safety behaviours in more detail in Part Two, Section 4, but for now try writing down here some of the safety behaviours you think you may use.

_____

_____

_____

_____

Three effects of safety behaviours

The diagram on page 89 shows that there are three ways in which using safety behaviours can help to create vicious cycles.

Confirming your underlying assumptions

The arrow leading towards the top of the diagram shows how using safety behaviours means that the same types of situations will continue to trigger the problem. They confirm your underlying assumptions as well as reinforcing the impression that you have got to keep safe, or something bad might happen.

If you always take action to keep yourself safe, including when that is not necessary, this teaches you to go on taking protective action. It prevents you learning that the situations from which you are trying to protect yourself are harmless, and that the actions are not useful. It's a bit like hanging up garlic to keep vampires at bay and then imagining that because you haven't seen any vampires the garlic is doing its job!

Look at the safety behaviours you have listed above. Describe here how they may confirm your assumptions and prevent you growing or changing.

_____

_____

_____

Focusing your attention inwards

The second problem with safety behaviours is that they focus your attention inwards, and make you increasingly self-aware and self-conscious. This is shown by the arrow in the diagram from safety behaviours to the central circle. When you are very self-conscious the situation seems even more threatening.

Avoiding eye contact by keeping your eyes turned down (a safety behaviour) makes you aware of what is going on inside and prevents you finding out more about what is going on around you. So you cannot tell when it is safe to look up again, and the situation continues to feel dangerous. Safety behaviours such as failing to look directly at people also tend to attract attention, and becoming aware of this increases your self-consciousness further, so they actually make the situation worse.

Does your safety behaviour make you more self-conscious? Describe what happens here.

_____

_____

_____

_____

Increasing the signs and symptoms of anxiety

The third way in which safety behaviours link up with other reactions is that they can increase your signs and symptoms of anxiety rather than reduce them. This is shown by the line drawn along the bottom of the diagram. They can increase your levels of tension, nervousness, shakiness or embarrassment.

For example, tensing yourself up and trying to hold yourself steady makes you shake more, not less. Trying to make sure that you are not being boring makes it harder, not easier, to think of anything interesting to say. It makes you more tense and nervous and less able to come across naturally.

Have you noticed that your anxiety symptoms become worse when you practise your safety behaviours? Describe what happens here.

_____

_____

_____

_____

How do the signs and symptoms of anxiety, for example the bodily changes such as heart thumping, sweating and trembling, and the feelings of nervousness, fit in to the Clark and Wells theory?

The model shows that when you see a social situation as threatening or dangerous, this produces signs and symptoms of anxiety such as shaky hands. This increases your self-consciousness as others might notice the fact that you are shaking. Then the situation seems even more threatening or dangerous to you. If others notice the shaking they might judge you on the basis of this 'weakness'.

It's worth remembering...

Symptoms of social anxiety are often the things that socially anxious people notice most, and that they are most worried about. However, symptoms start to disappear when you change the thoughts and behaviour that keep them going.

Why the Clark and Wells theory helps overcome social anxiety

This theory identifies three things that keep social anxiety going:

- Patterns of thinking

- Safety behaviours

- Self-consciousness.

The theory is also helpful because it explains why social anxiety does not disappear despite all the situations you have been in that have turned out to be less bad than you feared. There are two reasons for this.

1 A one-sided view

The first reason social anxiety doesn't disappear is because when you are socially anxious you focus your attention inwards, onto your inner experience – onto your own thoughts and sensations. This leaves less attention over for finding out what is really going on.

You end up with a one-sided or biased view of the situations that trouble you. You know all about how it feels from your own perspective but little about how it seems from other people's point of view.

2 The lucky escape

The second reason why social anxiety doesn't go away is because your efforts to keep safe, even when they are not entirely successful, leave you feeling that things would have been worse if you had not tried to protect yourself. You feel that you have only narrowly missed a 'real' disaster; it is as if your social life is a series of lucky escapes.

Let's look at some real-life stories below to see how the model works in practice.

Examples of the main processes that keep social anxiety going

CASE STUDY: Nathan

Nathan is thirty-five and suffers from social anxiety. He was the youngest child of rather elderly parents, and he had two brothers seven and ten years older than him, who teased him mercilessly throughout his childhood.

Nathan grew up with the impression that they were the 'real' family and that he was the afterthought. All his efforts to join in, to copy his brothers and to belong, failed to change their attitude towards him.

However, Nathan greatly admired his brothers, who were more successful than he was in many of the ways that mattered to him, and he assumed that 'they were right and he was wrong'. He ended up thinking of himself as 'different', and this belief became stronger after an episode of being bullied at secondary school.

Let's see what happens when Nathan joins a group of people who are having a drink. Think about how Nathan behaves based on what you've learnt about cycles of social anxiety. Try to identify:

- Nathan's underlying assumptions and beliefs (for a reminder of what these are see page 57).

- His self-awareness cycles (see page 91).

- The danger he sees in the situation (see page 54).

- His negative automatic thoughts (see page 56).

- His safety behaviours (see page 16).

- The signs and symptoms of his anxiety (see page 6).

As soon as he joins the group Nathan finds himself thinking 'I'm not going to be able to think of anything to say', 'I'm going to do something wrong', 'I can't come over well'. He feels that he does not belong, and that he is different from other people. He starts to feel threatened, and this makes it hard for him to behave normally. Immediately he focuses in on himself. He becomes aware that his mind has gone blank. He notices every silence in the conversation. He cannot grasp exactly what everyone is talking about. He avoids looking directly at people because he feels embarrassed, and wants to hide this from them. At the same time he makes a big effort to ensure that what he says does make sense.

But while his mind is preoccupied in this way it is hard for him to listen to what other people are saying. He becomes increasingly uncertain about whether what he has just said did make sense, and as this goes on he feels the tension inside him start to build. As the anxiety increases he feels hot, fearful and panicky. It becomes hard to concentrate or to 'think straight', and he has the sense that he is talking nonsense. This makes him super-aware of everything he says. He is also embarrassed and humiliated by his anxiety symptoms, and this makes him feel even more self-conscious.

The diagram below shows how Nathan's experience fits the model of social anxiety we've been looking at.

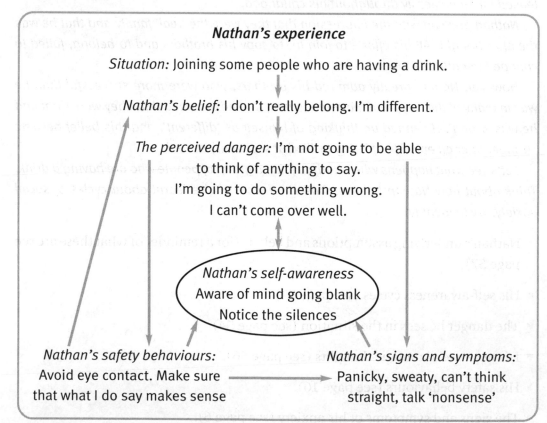

Nathan's experience

Situation: Joining some people who are having a drink.

Nathan's belief: I don't really belong. I'm different.

The perceived danger: I'm not going to be able to think of anything to say.
I'm going to do something wrong.
I can't come over well.

Nathan's self-awareness
Aware of mind going blank
Notice the silences

Nathan's safety behaviours:
Avoid eye contact. Make sure that what I do say makes sense

Nathan's signs and symptoms:
Panicky, sweaty, can't think straight, talk 'nonsense'

The effect on Nathan

Regardless of whether he eventually calms down, regardless of how the situation develops, and regardless of whether anyone notices how Nathan feels inside, he will come away with the impression that situations like this one are potential sources of danger. Even though he tried to keep himself under control, and tried hard to say the right sorts of things, he ended up feeling 'different' again, convinced that others too would think that he did not really belong.

Nathan's assumptions have been confirmed by these inward-looking, cyclical processes. This is despite the fact that other people in the group may have been totally uncritical in their responses to him. Many of them probably know what social anxiety is like. They may also have enjoyed his company.

The part played by vicious cycles in keeping social anxiety going is very important. Let's look at some more examples of cycles involving safety behaviours, self-consciousness, beliefs and assumptions.

It's worth remembering…

Recognizing vicious cycles and how they work in practice for you is one of the first steps to take in overcoming social anxiety.

Examples of maintenance cycles involving safety behaviours

CASE STUDY: Sue

Sue was someone who blushed easily. The fear that she would blush was never far from her mind, and she developed a habit of hiding behind her hair. Whenever she felt at risk she let her hair fall in front of her face, and tried to avoid looking at people. Underneath this protective screen she felt she glowed like a beacon. Her mind was occupied with monitoring how red she thought she looked, and awareness of the people around her. Were they looking? Had they noticed? What were they thinking?

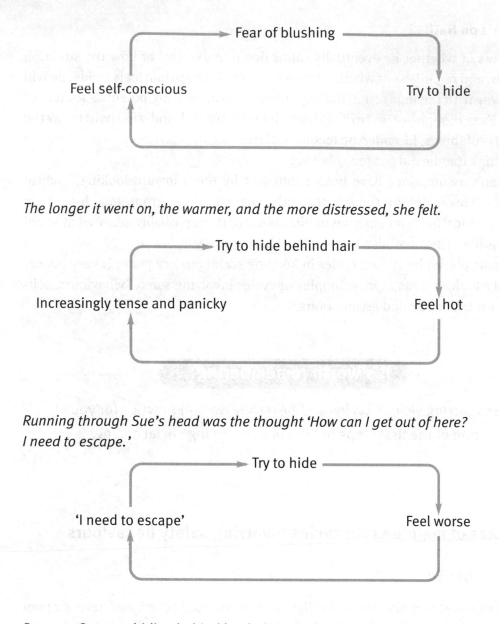

The longer it went on, the warmer, and the more distressed, she felt.

Running through Sue's head was the thought 'How can I get out of here? I need to escape.'

Because Sue was hiding behind her hair it was hard to attract her attention, so other people had to look closely at her to see whether or not they were getting a response.

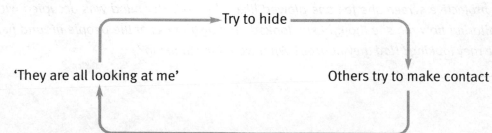

After the event, Sue thought that it might have been even worse if she had not tried to keep herself safe.

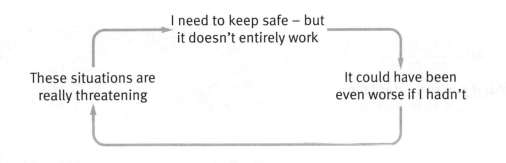

I need to keep safe – but
it doesn't entirely work

These situations are
really threatening

It could have been
even worse if I hadn't

It seems only sensible to avoid situations that really are threatening or dangerous. Sue decides in the end that the best thing for her is to keep herself safe by withdrawing a bit more.

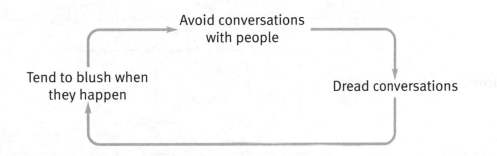

Avoid conversations
with people

Tend to blush when
they happen

Dread conversations

Do your safety behaviours create cycles that keep your social anxiety going? Think of a recent situation in which you were socially anxious and complete the diagram below. Use Sue's diagram above as a guide.

The sign or symptom of social anxiety you find embarrassing:

_____

Your safety behaviour:

_____

_____

_____

How you felt during the situation:

_____

_____

_____

What you were thinking:

_____

_____

_____

How people around you behaved:

_____

_____

_____

How you felt afterwards:

_____

_____

_____

Maintenance cycles

Blushing is only one, and one of the most obvious, symptoms of social anxiety. Similar maintenance cycles are likely to be involved whenever you use safety behaviours to reduce the risks of social encounters and hide embarrassing signs or symptoms of your anxiety.

For instance, if it feels risky to express an opinion, or to reveal personal things about yourself, then other people will probably at some stage ask you personal questions. This is not because they are cruel and insensitive, but because eventually they want to know more about you, and that includes knowing more about your personal likes, dislikes, activities, experiences or history. If they want to be friendly, or to get to know you, they may ask you precisely the kinds of questions that you find it difficult to answer, and they may repeat them if you fail to respond.

The cycles show that using safety behaviours, trying to keep yourself safe and to reduce the perceived risk, is an understandable thing to want to do, but it is counter-productive.

It's worth remembering...

Keeping safe prevents you learning that there is no need to keep safe. The situation is not really dangerous, it just seems to be so.

Examples of maintenance cycles in which self-consciousness plays a central part

CASE STUDY: Tim

Tim had always been shy. For example, at school he kept his head down in class hoping that he would not be asked to answer questions. It had taken him nearly 18 months to find the courage to respond to the warmth and friendliness of someone he had met at work. The relationship he now had with her was precious to him. In fact he could hardly believe his luck, and in the back of his mind he feared that at some stage, in some way, it would all go wrong. She would find someone more interesting or attractive and that would be the end of it. He was constantly worried that he was not good enough for her – that in some way he would fail to come up to the mark.

When he was with her, Tim became preoccupied with what he was saying. He was aware that he said little, and worried that what he did say might be boring.

Worry about being boring

Aware of saying little

Self-preoccupation

Focusing on himself meant that he knew more about what he felt like inside than about how he was really coming over – than about what was actually happening.

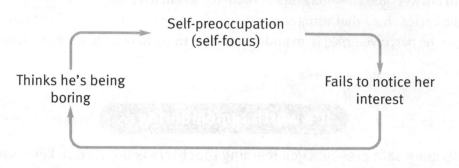

He knows that he has always been shy, and that this made his teenage years extremely painful. The situation reminds him of bad times in the past.

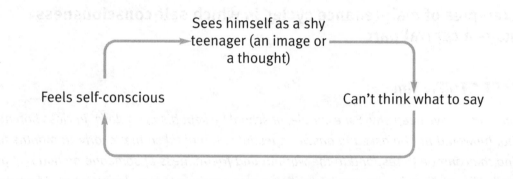

It is easy to see from these examples why self-awareness has been described as the engine that drives social anxiety. Being self-aware makes the situation worse because it produces the wrong kind of information. Being pre-occupied with yourself provides information about what is going on inside you, which you use as information about how you appear to others. It fills your mind with information (and images) about yourself and leaves you lacking in accurate information about others, and how they react to you.

Does self-consciousness keep your social anxiety going? Think about a recent situation in which you were anxious and complete the list opposite. Use Tim's diagram above as a guide.

The situation:

_____

_____

Your worry about how you would behave in the situation:

_____

_____

_____

What you thought about how you did behave during the situation:

_____

_____

_____

Any memories or images the situation brought to mind:

_____

_____

_____

How you actually behaved:

_____

_____

_____

Examples of maintenance cycles involving beliefs and assumptions

CASE STUDY: Rachel and Tony

Rachel and Tony came from a family of shy, retiring people. The family motto, had they had one, might have been 'Do not intrude'. Both of them were friendly people at heart and neither of them had had any great problems getting on with people at school. They *had been ready to cooperate with others and joined in the usual range of joint activities. Being likeable people, they were able to make friends in this situation; but later on, both of them became progressively isolated and socially anxious.*

Rachel's confidence was shaken when she went to college, leaving all the people she knew behind. She found it hard to make new friends, and she began to think that the other students did not like her or want her around.

Tony stayed near to the family home where he had found a good job, but gradually his friends moved away, leaving him, as he thought, the odd one out. He started to spend a lot of time on his own, listening to music or playing computer games, and became increasingly isolated and lonely.

Rachel

Rachel was not really shy; she just assumed that 'you shouldn't put yourself forward', and that 'if others want you with them, they will let you know'. So she never made the first move, or started a conversation with someone she did not know, or joined a group of people who were already talking to each other. Going into the huge college canteen became the ordeal that activated these assumptions, and produced a situation that appeared to confirm them.

Rachel's assumption: If others want you, they'll make that clear.

Rachel's thoughts: I'll be a bother to someone; I'll be in the way.

Rachel's safety behaviour: Chooses to sit somewhere on her own, out of the way.

The result: Other people are not sure she wants to join in, and leave her alone. Rachel ends up thinking that the other students don't like her: if they had done so, they would have made it clear.

Tony

Tony was spending most weekends alone, and had done so for many months. Then he heard that some of the people he had known at school were getting together for a drink in the local pub. He thought of going, and wondered why no one had contacted him. He assumed that they would have done so if they really wanted him to be there. By now he knew, and supposed they did also, that he was the odd one out. But nevertheless he felt lonely enough to want to make the effort to join in.

Tony's assumption: If I was OK, people would keep in touch.

Tony's thought: I'm different. I'm weird.

Tony's safety behaviour: Tony decides to go to the pub, but sits on the edge of the group because that feels safer. However, he feels self-conscious, and worried that others will think he is odd. He finds it difficult to talk, is hesitant about saying much about himself, and he feels increasingly embarrassed as time goes on.

The result: People talk to each other, but not to him. Tony feels left out, odd and weird, and the less he says the less people talk to him.

The cycles involved here are quite complex, and may have many more steps in them than the simpler ones illustrated earlier. Also, Rachel's and Tony's cases show that the exact meaning of similar assumptions, and the precise effect that they have, differ from person to person. They both started with the family view that you should not intrude on other people, but ended in rather different places. No two people are exactly the same, even though the process that keeps the social anxiety going is based on the same beliefs and assumptions and has the same, cyclical form.

Do your beliefs and assumptions keep your social anxiety going? Think of a recent difficult situation and answer the questions below using Tony and Rachel's stories to guide you.

The situation:

_____

_____

_____

_____

My assumption:

_____

_____

_____

My thoughts:

_____

_____

_____

_____

My safety behaviour:

_____

_____

_____

The result:

_____

_____

_____

Other kinds of maintenance cycles

The Clark and Wells model of social anxiety focuses on what happens when you encounter one of the situations that you fear. The cycles explain why your anxiety persists in these particular situations.

Similar cycles can be set in motion in other ways too:

● Before entering a situation that you expect to find socially difficult

● When thinking about the situation after it is over

● When the behaviour of other people appears to confirm your fears.

Let's look at each of these cycles in more detail.

Anticipation or dread

Many socially anxious people worry for days in advance about events like meetings or parties or encounters with people who provoke their worst symptoms. During this time they tend to think about things that could go wrong and to dwell on possible (imaginary) disasters.

The effects of anticipatory anxiety, or dread, are relatively easy to recognize. Worrying that you will shake, or say something foolish, makes you anxious, and the anxiety makes you nervous and tense ahead of time, which is enough to set the social anxiety going.

Or it diverts your mind on to worrying about what other people think of you, which in turn makes any encounter with them seem even more threatening. The longer this goes on, the more likely such disasters seem, and the worse the anxiety gets.

No wonder avoidance seems sometimes to be the best option – the only possible way of keeping safe from potential catastrophe.

Do you dread particular events or encounters? Does this make your anxiety worse? Describe your experience here.

After the event: the post mortem

When thinking about a social situation after the event is over, socially anxious people tend to perform a kind of post mortem. We looked at this earlier on page 18. Unfortunately your analysis tends to confirm your own biased view of what 'really happened'.

If you felt hot and flustered you assume that others noticed and judged you 'accordingly'. The symptoms that were so distressing at the time sometimes flood back again when you remember what happened – usually because of the assumptions that you are making. So you tend to think that other people noticed the symptoms, or thought badly about you if they did notice. Or you decide that any social difficulty that occurred was all your fault, as if you were entirely and solely responsible for how things went at the time.

As we have already seen, socially anxious people, because of their tendency to become preoccupied with themselves, often leave situations with incomplete or inaccurate information about what really went on. The post mortem is counterproductive because it can only be based on this inaccurate data. Dwelling on things after the event becomes another way of continuing the problem. It leads you to conclude that your assumptions were correct even though you have not really tested them out. It often makes you feel bad about yourself too, so undermines your confidence and self-esteem.

Do you dwell on events after they are over? Think about how that makes you feel about yourself? About other people? About your ability to change in ways that would help? Describe what you think you do here.

When awkwardness spreads

But what if being socially anxious creates real difficulties? What if the person with the social anxiety is right (or partly right) about what other people are thinking about them?

Sometimes it does happen that the awkwardness or shyness of the person who is socially anxious appears to spread to others. Someone who is anxious may give the impression of being cold and distant, and other people may then respond to them in colder and more distancing ways than they otherwise would have done.

When one side of a social interaction falters, the other may do so also. When one person cannot think of anything to say, the conversation may quickly dry up. This cycle is played out between socially anxious people and those involved with them, who may not initially be unfriendly or critical but who may appear to be so once the effects of the anxiety have become apparent.

The cause of the spreading awkwardness is not to do with the inadequacy, weakness or unacceptability of one of the people involved. It is rather a consequence of the social anxiety, and the effects of this anxiety on the interaction. The way to overcome this problem is to learn how to break the main vicious cycles mentioned above.

How to bring about change

The model of social anxiety we have been looking at shows that, once the patterns of thinking involved in social anxiety are in place, the central process that keeps the problem going is a cycle. So the main strategy used in treatment is to break the cycles: to interrupt them, and change the patterns that keep them going.

Two of the most important types of cycle are:

1 Those involving self-consciousness

2 Those involving safety behaviours.

Working on these two problems can sometimes be enough to solve your problem and to set in motion the processes that build confidence in a lasting way.

Sometimes additional work has to be done on the longer-standing beliefs and assumptions. You may need to find out whether they reflect an accurate or a biased view of the world, and to see whether there are alternative and more helpful perspectives that fit the facts better. Changing old habits of thinking may take longer.

Part Two of this workbook will give you practical strategies to help you change your habits of thinking and behaviour in order to overcome social anxiety.
But for now, well done. You've come a long way in understanding exactly what social anxiety is, what causes it and what keeps the problem going. Understanding those three things are essential in finally overcoming social anxiety.

Summary

1   Theories and models are useful because they explain how to understand social anxiety, and what keeps it going. They also show ways to overcome it.

2   A number of different cycles keep the problem going.

3   The cycles involve three levels of thinking: your level of self-awareness, your level of negative automatic thoughts, and your level of underlying assumptions and beliefs.

4   Cycles involving self-consciousness are very important. Focusing attention on yourself means that you come away from the situations you fear with a biased view of yourself, your performance and the way that others see you.

5   Cycles involving safety behaviours prevent people learning that social situations are not truly dangerous.

6   Long-standing assumptions and beliefs keep the problem going because they determine the ways in which you see and interpret social situations.

7   Breaking cyclical patterns of behaviour that may have continued for a long time is an excellent way of building confidence. Becoming more confident helps people to relax and to be themselves when interacting with others.

Thoughts and Reflections

Thoughts and Reflections

Thoughts and Reflections

Thoughts and Reflections